All Eyes On U.S.

And Yes We Can

Mel C. Igbokwe

authorHOUSE®

AuthorHouse™
1663 Liberty Drive, Suite 200
Bloomington, IN 47403
www.authorhouse.com
Phone: 1-800-839-8640

First published by AuthorHouse 7/1/2009

ISBN: 978-1-4389-8199-4 (sc)
ISBN: 978-1-4389-8200-7 (hc)

Library of Congress Control Number: 2009905175

Printed in the United States of America
Bloomington, Indiana

This book is printed on acid-free paper.

Contents

About the Author

Mel C. Igbokwe, originally from Nigeria, was born in November 11, 1951. He has been a regular contributor to the yearly journal for Amuzi Development Fund U.S.A. Inc; — a not for profit organization since 2001. His inspiring essays and articles have passion for the organization's campaign for funds to rebuild his rural community's primary school that was ones owned by a church and later taken over and neglected by the state and local governments.

His guidance, his dual exposure and perception in the America and African culture, religious believes and practices, his attention in politics, all provide his readers unparalleled information and knowledge which would make their hairs stand on end. He trained for computer networks, also a phlebotomist; he splits his time working with the Texas oncology and exports computer hardware. He is married with four children, and lives in Texas.

Prologue

"On every thorn, delightful wisdom grows, in every rill a sweet instruction flows," said Edward Young, the English poet and author of "Night Thoughts."

My book is written with a flair and creativity covering a wide range of interesting, entertaining, and informative social, political, and religious issues, some of them controversial—drawing illustrations and offering opinions through African and American points of views.

Robert Frost, the American professor of poetry said: "For me the initial delight is in the surprise of remembering something I didn't know I knew." There is little doubt you can do the same with the information I have written herein.

In the rush of life we tend to forget the significance of events, the places and the times they took place. In this instance Henry Cisneros, a professor of environmental studies and notable Hispanic activist, said: "Americans are a can-do people, an enthusiastic people, and a problem-solving people. And when given a direction and given a plan, they'll sign on."

Within the spirit of the American way of life, you will learn from my book the importance of problem solving, gathered from the different situations of my upbringing in Nigeria and how the experience in tackling some of my village problems prepared me to take an active part in the 2008 U.S. presidential election. It's all about sacrifice and dedication.

Also in my book, you will find out about the imperfection of man in all segments of life and the enormous gratitude we owe the police, even when they make mistakes.

On both sides of the Atlantic, I narrated my shocking encounters with police and think that sharing them will instill in you an enormous sense of humility and better judgments because one who understands a good deal displays a greater simplicity of character than one who understands the least.

If anyone wonders how history should honor all our heroes and heroines, my book jogs your mind on how not to forget them. This book calls on every age to respect their foremost ambassadors in the world—their mothers and fathers, dead or living.

To all, you will gain knowledge in my prediction that American success in alternate and renewable energy is likely to create catastrophic effects throughout the oil-producing nations of the world.

America leads the world and therefore is too mighty to fail in whatever it does. America is the most generous and compassionate nation in the world. We have no choice in the position of our greatness and in our responsibility to take the world to a resounding moral and successful path.

In our ideals to harvest the return of our internal energies you will discover from the start of the book and all the way to the end, how to fervently respond to calls when the chemistry of our imagination and our understanding are decisively not in doubt. You will no doubt be excited with the spell of information which will enrich your knowledge about the truth in our individual lives when we should follow our instinct at one point and at some other times, when our instinct follows us.

That is not all; you will find documentary evidence of the world's curiosity and inestimable excitement for America in decades and how the attention exploded in the 2008 U.S. presidential election.

Just like me, you cannot thank your stars enough to be an American. From every conceivable record, America has done a great deal for the world. They have answered almost all the world's emergency calls. In my book I laid out a more realistic approach in lifting Africa up, not by the old system of pumping endless cash into endless dark tunnels, but through support of reliable and dependable sources of energy so that the people can work and walk themselves up to end their long dependence on foreign aid.

To view our world from two windows seeing the sun shine on one part of the globe while darkness falls on the other is as good as to be in two places at a time. And through the gift of daylight on a fraction of the earth and the darkness which sends the rest of the world to sleep we learn a great deal from the people who live through them.

Furthermore, you will find out in my book about the endemic siphoning of African assets into foreign banks. Such reprehensible acts have crippled African progress for many years. Therefore if America helps to wage war against such corruption and in repatriating Africa's wealth in Europe, America and other countries, Africa might one day see some rays of hope and development shine across its land.

Finally, you would be convinced we have urgent need to talk about the limitations in Africa, to write about them, and campaign about them and to put Africa on the cradle of civilization which will eventually lift a huge burden off American shoulders in foreign aid because money not spent, is money saved.

Mel C. Igbokwe
Fort Worth, Texas
April 2009.

Chapter 1

Tribute to our Heroes and Heroines

Modern societies do not forget their defenders; they respect and idolize them. Not honoring our champions in strident voice is deliberately defaming history. To excavate those names, recite their contributions, and give them a position in history is the right thing to do, and must be done without delay.

I look back at the sacrifices that our predecessors made to uplift the wellbeing of our communities and thought it is wise for us to give them a place in history, because they:

> Labored under the scourge of the sun without good water, transportation, and electricity.
> Made hoes for their farms, bricks for our schools, chairs for our churches, and shovels for our roads.
> Were good in political expedience and judgments.
> Hung the Legion of Mary on our necks for safety; such a noble gift no one else would give.
> Made us coats of many colors that fit, and, with a school band, made our learning musical and fun.

Primed the vitamins and minerals of our generation;
nothing could have been wiser.

From every perspective, ancestors deserve our credit, because some of them put their lives on the line for our community; others sacrificed their time, and the rest, their priceless resources. We should remember them, not less than we commit to memory the victims of September 11, 2001, here in America when 19 Islamist terrorists affiliated with al-Qaeda attacked us.

We should also do the same to those whose voices and proverbs have fashioned our morals in our early infancy.

Records should be kept of the individual whose contributions in policies, decision making, and funding of our community projects including those who raised the image of our people. Top on the list is Bob Miga, owner manager of the Strangers Band. His "Love Rock" music was a great heat in the early 1970, and it added gleaming respect to our dear community. Also the first Amuzi school bandleader, uncle Bartholomew, alias 'Aka.'

I challenge our history scholars to put our past on record. We owe it to our people and have no excuse to shift the responsibility to the next generation.

We are the vitamins and "minerals of our generation. If we are not grateful for our natural gifts of wisdom and opportunities, we are less likely to value them, and if we don't value them, we are unlikely to make every effort to preserve and to develop toward excellence.

As the world swells around us today, all of us should be recommending plausible plans that could be of help to our communities. Computer education programs that could keep idle minds busy and remove them from theft, drugs is one way. How about libraries for expansion of knowledge to replace hijacking and abduction?

Even with our slim resources, we can give priority to projects that promise great returns. There's no doubt great passion brings great effort. We should not forget a journey of a thousand miles starts with a step, and then another step, and so on.

Africa is not modernized because there is a lack of educational materials and workshops. Because there is lack of exposure, freedom of expression and new ideas in Africa, the world continues to pull away further and further away from Africa. The wrong choices and actions Africa takes digs her deeper into tunnels of darkness and instability.

Instead of modern science, which could earn good jobs and put her on the world map for self-sufficiency, we have cold and crude ideas of the 15th century Africa, seen in their movie productions.

As unbelievable as it was, we had news coming out of Nigeria about a goat detained regarding armed robbery Friday January 23, 2009. LAGOS (Reuters) stating that Police in Nigeria are holding a goat on suspicion of attempted armed robbery. Vigilantes took the black and white beast to the police saying it was an armed robber who had used black magic to transform himself into a goat to escape arrest after trying to steal a Mazda 323.

"The group of vigilante men came to report that while they were on patrol they saw some hoodlums attempting to rob a car. They pursued them. However one of them escaped while the other turned into a goat," Kwara state police spokesman Tunde Mohammed told Reuters by telephone: "We cannot confirm the story, but the goat is in our custody. We cannot base our information on something mystical. It is something that has to be proved scientifically, that a human being turned into a goat," he said.

Reuters reported that belief in witchcraft is widespread in parts of Nigeria, Africa's most populous nation, and that residents came to the police station to see the goat.

This kind of story and news will go on in the minds of the people. Soon, in order to attract clients, someone hundreds of miles away is going to take advantage of the news and say he is the traditional medicine man who can make a man turn into a goat.

The police officer who said that the case needed scientific proof made a wild suggestion because I do not think such a laboratory with electricity could be found within the country.

It's frustrating to hear people still believe that every death that occurs in the family is perpetuated by a family member through a kind of traditional potion or voodoo that still flourishes in Brazil, Africa, Trinidad, Jamaica, Cuba, and Haiti. It is also irritating to watch their movies promote clear unscientific belief and to see their practices sever family relationships. These are stumbling blocks to progressive thinking and application.

You wonder how people, who have neither medical laboratories nor genuine medications, or rationalized doctors, and regulatory bodies to guide against malpractices, could be hopeful of a better health care.

This year, February 2009 a friend in Africa who is allergic to Septrin medication was told by villagers who referred him to traditional medicine doctor that his enemies had poisoned him with rashes. Because of the information, he suffered both physical and psychological trauma.

"Fears are but voices airy; whispering harm where harm is not." –William Wordsworth.

To demystify his fears, I called him and my first question to him was whether he remembered taking any antibiotics medication days prior to the outburst of his rashes. In his own words, he said, "Septrin." Then I told him he must have suffered from medication reaction. My over the telephone diagnostics and suggestion that he meets a medical doctor for antidote treatment helped him in his healing process.

In 2004, a boy, his name, Valentine 16 years old then, whose sister baby-sat my children in 1988 through the first quarter of 1990, came to me with great anxiety and said to me: "Uncle, someone has just sent stroke to my mother while she was with other women, celebrating the birth of a baby."

"Valentine, come and sit down here with me for a minute," I said. And he did. Then, I asked him if he knew the person that sent the stroke and he answered, "Yes, it must be one of my uncles, who has not been treating us well since our father died." Then I asked him if the stroke was sent through the post office or by e-mail. He was quiet and looked steadily into my eyes. After about a minute silence, I explained to him a few things that can cause stoke: High cholesterol, stress, high blood pressure, aortic aneurysm, embolism and so on. None of these can be sent to anyone. Humorously, I asked for anyone to sends the stroke to me, and added I would mail it back to sender.

I further demanded for someone to introduce me to the native doctor, whom I would pay to teach me the supernatural power of sending stroke to at least, Osama Bin Laden. If I learned how to send the stroke or hired someone to do so, it would at least stop US and our allies from fighting in search of Bin Laden and his vicious partners in terrorism around the world. No one could give me answer to my request.

When my listener was convinced I made a good point I asked him not to pay attention to a belief that has neither laboratory nor transcript could be investigated. If Americans and suffer the same stroke without pointing fingers at anyone to be responsible for it, it therefore makes no sense to dwell on myth.

When he left, an elderly uncle was already waiting for me and certainly overheard my discussion with the boy. He did not waste time in jumping at me on the issue, critical of my opinion. So I told him that I might not be correct in what I have said and that all I wanted him to do was take up an assignment to introduce to the a native doctor whom I would pay some money to teach me how to send a stroke to someone and also how to be a rainmaker.

First, I promised him I would appear on CNN if ever I could have such powers to make the rain and the potion to send stroke. Bin Laden would be my first target.

When I brought up the subject of rainmaking and told him about the type of dry weather conditions we have in Texas and how seriously farmers need rain for their farms he was convinced I indeed need an answer to it.

In reply, he told me traditional medicine doesn't cross the ocean because of the evil spirits that control the oceans. That argument had no muscles.

I insisted I would be flying above the ocean in aircraft, not by ship or boat to overcome the effect of the ocean. He replied, "Young people like you don't understand because of our attainment of the western culture."

Then I argued, if the tablets of Codeine, Advil, and antibiotics from foreign countries can reach Africa through the air and not by swimming across the oceans without being deactivated, why would anyone think the "brilliant science of rainmaking and sending of stroke" through the air can not make it to Africa? He didn't say a word.

I asked uncle, is it possible that the gods of the sea would get into fight with the gods of the sky as the airplane delivers its goods? Again, he said that I won't understand and there I ended our argument, affirming that a science that has no apparatus, procedure, or proof is like a house that has neither address nor directions on how to get to it. I would not like to live in such a home, I concluded.

What surprises me is that people, educated men and women, who you think could have led the illiterate ones to good reasoning are the ones who are strong in the fetish belief. "I have recently been examining all the known superstitions of the world, and do not find in our particular superstition (Christianity) one redeeming feature. They are all alike founded on fables and mythology." Thomas Jefferson.

Chapter 2

Our Choice to Be

After the November 4 2008 US election, global reaction echoed from every part of the world. Mostafa Eqbali, a 54-year-old merchant in downtown Tehran said, "Let me tell you that now I believe in American democracy." "Honestly, I did not think that Obama would be president. I thought that the invisible hands of the big trusts and cartels would not allow a black man to be president of the United States," he continued.

"It is a true democracy," Mosavi, a former political prisoner, said. "A black man is victorious. It is important that a man with the middle name Hussein and with Islamic roots is in the White House. He addressed the needs of the poor and grass-roots. He is one of us."

Already there are slight changes taking place in the hearts and minds of the people of the world; how long that will hold on is anyone's guess. Nevertheless, the world looks for a virtual leadership, a leader that doesn't have arrogance in his resume and a nation that is pro-peace and not a threat to world peace.

Through his point of view and his statements about not only talking to our friends, but also our enemies, the world may once again look onto the United States of America for salvation. That's why everyone teared up. That's why we think there's something unique and hidden in all humans.

Even though the world has drifted so much apart and we're all finding our own little spaces inside it, we know that when our tears fall or our smiles spread across our faces, we come to one another because no matter where the crazy world takes us, not so much will change to the point where we're not all still one body and one soul.

The way we respond to natural adversities around the world, for example the 2004 tsunami in Southeast Asia makes the world see us as an exemplary of character and goodness that nature ever had.

Despite our humanitarian spirits we find out that not everyone loves us and the reason for that may be one or several things.

There's not much we can do to know what individual mind thinks of us. But, we do know that a country is loved or hated through the posture and especially the utterances of its leader, not through the action of her citizens.

With the successful election of President Obama the world heaved a sigh of great relief. We couldn't ask for more, having been touched in the same spirit of mankind to end all hatred and wars.

Our thoughts and tears are the reservoirs of our sorrows as well as our joys, and they glue the world together as one.

Whether it is the Rwanda massacre in Central Africa, the "9/11 disaster" in the United States of America, the tsunami of southeast Asia, or the election of a an African American president in United States, in all these episodes, we felt realistic international energy of heart and mind not only fused together, but steered our human feelings to a common purpose. Shalom! Shalom! (Peace! Peace!).

A journalist from South Africa wrote: "Damn, I love Americans. Just when you've written them off as hopeless, as a nation in decline, they turn around and do something extraordinary, which tells you why the United States of America is still the greatest nation on earth. But too, what is happening in America and Kenya hold lessons for politicians everywhere, and South Africa would do well to take heed" www.thoughtleader.co.za

The things that matter the most in our lives are down-to-earth. They are those moments when we profoundly touch one another, when we are intimately there in the most thoughtful and caring way, feeling one another's pain and cheering in one another's success.

If anyone wants to achieve a meaningful community project, one would expect part of his strength to come from his critics. To borrow Shakespeare's philosophy: "...The eye does not see itself except by reflection." Therefore, if you are really attentive to good judgments, you must keep your critics in view with the aim of improving yourself to the benefit of history.

In my closing remark at the Amuzi Development Fund (ADF) — a non-profit organization — convention in New York in 2002, I presented a visual image of a three-level-stepladder with upward and downward arrows with the purpose of prompting the audience to choose a direction. The idea was for us to focus on how to send down the rain of sustenance and delight, because our choice to be is in reality our chance to win and make history. I also share in President Obama's declaration that we all will be judged by what we build, not what we destroy.

It is nature's design not ours, that we emigrants share the understanding of two continents, Africa and North America, and of 20th and 21st centuries in our lifetime. Of the two continents, one has vision and the other, none. Also, one is democratic and the other lives under the shadow of democracy. In the continents of North America and Africa, where we, immigrants have dual citizenship despite the difficulties of the global economic crunch, we see respect for the law and positive changes as shown in the last election. Ushering in an African-American president is an idea worthy of our export to Africans for them to embrace.

We have the privilege to respond to nature's generosity of spirit by sowing the seeds that will sprout the growth and development of mankind.

We know we need change; there's little doubt about our capability of being a revolutionary "dream team" in our towns and villages because our elders say, If termites could build towers as tall as the Empire State Building out of their sheer saliva and mud, we can do better out of a fraction of our breakfast budget to rehabilitate some schools that would include a library and employment of instructors to teach children the four basic skills of how to read, write, understand, and how to remember.

To actualize this dream than show off with, "Hey men" back home is not helping out. So far we have had enough prompts to act, at our back and in front of us. Making my individual judgment, I recall a disagreement that I had with my father in mid May 1987, when he relentlessly pressured me to pay my levy for the remodeling of St. Jude's Catholic Church. Because I was unable and unwilling to pay the levy, I rebuked my father against his "old folks" change decision to spend extra money in a church that was already two times the size of many churches I had seen in England and Wales.

Instead of arguing, my father said to me, "Mel, if we finish building the church now, your own generation will focus on something else to do, something greater than what we are doing now."

I gave up my pessimistic position to modernizing the church and paid my levy a few months later.

Happily, today, I see the prophecy of my late father whirling in the heart of the very generation he had in mind, collaborating to lift the people to new highs.

Although, other communities around our hometown, Amuzi are involved in one project or the other to uplift the lifestyle of their people, we can make a spectacular splash in the growth of our hometown and be ahead of the game not only by building a surrogate school, but sponsoring accelerated reading to enhance the children's education.

With a modern library in our town, we can be sure the beneficiaries would be highly competitive in earning exclusive governmental positions and would do something positive for the next generation as my father thought of ours. I would reinforce that it's better to be ready for opportunities rather than to waste them.

Who knows how disintegrated the community and the environmental outlook of Amuzi would have been today without the foresight and the foundation of our predecessors toward investment in their children's education?

Those days are gone. The ideals have been replaced with the fights for traditional titles. The result has been disarray and people fleeing from that used to be a sincere and cherished community.

Back in the 1960s, our parents, in many ways, were in school with us. By that, I mean that St. Jude's school band was their literally timekeeper, which kept them side by side with the beginning and the end of our school session. Not many of them had transistor radios or wrist watches. The composition and vibration of our school band was a musical substitute they enjoyed from their paltry farms and local market squares.

They had two listening interludes in their daily lives so long as our school was in session. Whether our mothers were at their farms or at the market, buying and selling, hearing the band at the close of school day was such an air memo, which shoved them to quicken their pace back home to fix our lunch and, almost at the same time, our dinner before darkness took the sky.

Seeing us school children in straight lines during our morning parade and at the end of school day fascinated our parents a great deal. Definitely it accounted for the reason they made their weekly schedule correspond with our morning and end-of-school melodies. In a small community such as ours, the teacher, who was in charge of the band, enjoyed special recognition and was loved by all.

He later extended his music skills and entertainment to weddings and midnight ballroom dances within and beyond our community. That made us big-time snoopers as well.

But we couldn't see much through the cracks on the walls or partially opened doors. I guess they suffered from lack of fresh air; no electricity, there were nor fans. Tin-lanterns that radiated much heat as the afternoon rays of the tropical sun were largely used then.

All the wooden windows were shut and bolted; yet, if we were unfortunate to have been identified by any teacher we would be cold with the punishments that followed.

On the other hand, if we saw the cuffs of our teachers' trousers on the dancing floor, even if it was within a flash of a second, we were satisfied and it not only formed a headline news the following school day, Monday, it kept us busy the entire week mimicking what we imagined (we couldn't see them well) to be the teachers' style of dance, which made us feel special among our comrades

We were not in the parade alone. One day, Johnson, who was mentally sick, and lived close to the school, once said:

"I dance to the music and do the parade with the school also; but I 'don know why those in front of the parade are miraculously seen at the back, when there's order for round-about-turn!"

Johnson's question got very funny attention in the village and everyone, who heard it, laughed himself to ridicule.

It was and still is a million dollar question and has become a proverb in our community till today. It's not likely Johnson got the explanation to his question about the magic in switching positions at parade.

The school band and parade exercise were historic to our community. When the first band leader left town for another job with the state fire service, the community hired another man, named Achibong, from Calabar, a southeastern city of Nigeria, next to Cameroon. He received a monthly salary and enjoyed free housing and scholarship for his only son—Zik.

When the Nigerian-Biafra war erupted in 1966, it cost Amuzi their treasured school band and to this day has not been replaced—more than three decades after the civil war I have the feeling the ripples of the civil war will continue to be in our hallways until the band is re-established."

Isn't it a shame that our parents fashioned us with coats of many colors, but here we are, losing the path of the noble gifts?

Our people had the greatest moments of their lives in honoring many of us with huge send-off parties at the time we were leaving for the western world to improve ourselves.

It is disheartening that many of the people, people who donated to our success are dead or too old, too ill, or too hungry that they can't recognize us any more. They thought that one day, on our return; they would have broad smiles across their faces. Going back has not been easy.

Given the jungle nature of the environment, one might ask, if we shall ever get back to pomp and pageantry of the 1960's.

In between, I think prayers for them are not enough. What will be close to rewarding them adequately is giving something back to our community, in which they spent their entire lives. The question I have continued to ask and have fallen short of a meaningful answer is – what do we do? We know the majority never owned a car or had a chance to ride in one. The closest they got to an airplane was about 24,000 feet, watching from the ground.

Let us be stirred to act by the words of Benjamin Franklin: "If you fail to plan, then you plan to fail." In so many ways I think we will not fail, because I believe we are swollen with the pride of who we are as a people—a would-be polished and stylish community, too precious to be lost to the bleak winds of the earth.

We might be unaware that we should be children's role models. In that regard there are basic things we can do to form granite imprints in the minds of children who look to us for inspiration.

Something as trivial as holding a child, kissing him or her and taking a picture, can be a wonderful image to encourage children. Whether we are conscious of our reflection on the children's mind or not, we would be surprised that by night and by day all their eyes are set on us. It makes more sense when we lift and kiss not only our kids, but others.

Further to my reflection, many of us have experienced that teamwork is such a preeminence that we cannot afford to misplace in our mission to make a difference. Making the difference by doing little projects together goes a long way. Besides, it's those little things that add up to the big things that otherwise we could not have been capable of achieving individually.

Chapter 3

Youthful Pursuits and Entertainments

The common ground of St. Jude's Primary School and St Jude's church, Amuzi represented a mailbox of our daily attractions in our primary school years. We didn't need to open the packages to know what was in them; we trusted the power of our imaginations in sensing what each day would bring and fished them out as the flint catches fire.

Children everywhere yearn for outdoor activities. We didn't learn to swim because we neither had swimming pools nor streams around us otherwise we would be champions today if we got swimming practices.

We didn't have basketball courts and balls. But the girls played handballs, which was not so popular at the time. Parents were extremely overprotective of their teenage daughters. Any exposure, they feared, might land them into teen pregnancies, which was as unimaginable as it was shameful.

A mother could lose her parental custom and church sacraments if her daughter was out of luck with pregnant before marriage. By custom, fathers are blameless and so loose nothing.

If we weren't lucky to live close to the mission, where we had an open soccer field, I wonder what else we could have done to occupy our free moments and be as competitive as our counterparts, who were privileged with entertainment facilities, especially in the urban cities.

As much as children hunger after pizza, peanut butter, yogurts, macaroni and cheese, we wished to be left alone at play for hours on end, not bothered about anything else.

I recall that our parents didn't think about how important it was for us to drain our energies with outdoor games. Indoor amusements were well off the mark; our rooms were too narrow and too dark because of the tall and leafy cash crops that surrounded the houses. So, any form of in-house game was impossible, except, perhaps the hide and seek and we had virtually only 8-foot-by-10 foot dark room to do that.

Out in the open, we were able to play cricket, though, not without interruptions.

And as poor as we were, none of us could afford the ball alone. We therefore contributed our nickels and dimes to buy and collectively own the ball; yet our parents didn't want us in the game mainly, I think, for fear of injuries to our brittle legs. We played soccer when we grew a little bigger and our bones, a little stronger.

We lacked toys, swing sets, picnics tables and most things that could spark learning and creative activities in children. The open space within the school and church center had make-do facilities that growing children of our time needed for amusement and sports. We had soccer field for our soccer and track competition. It was not always safe to play in the field; sometimes we met with long and violent African pythons, maybe browsing and hunting for food.

Pine, mango, orange, and palm trees were there for our climbing skills. The trees were planted by Irish missionaries who administered our schools and our churches. We also had splendid varieties of flowers in front of the school; that made our nature studies worthwhile. Furthermore, we had a pineapple orchard on a quadrant, overlooking the teachers' residence, northwest of the playground. It was there we discovered that pineapple garden was home to rats, rabbits and hunting snakes. It was creepy to get in there carelessly. As much as we could, we avoided going there.

On the branches of those trees, we learned to climb and to compete with one another.

At the time when the trees were rich with ripe fruits, we were attracted to the mission a thousand times during the day, surveying the particular branches of ripe fruits we would pluck only at night so that our teachers wouldn't catch us in the act.

The resident teachers looked after the cash crops as hawks would watch over their eggs. Seeing us gaze at the branches of the mango trees was to give ourselves in for suspicion and ensuing punishment. We had a long and drawn out workshop on escape techniques that worked well for us.

To ward off risks, we chose to play our cricket ball around the mango and orange trees. We had just one ball at a time and if we kicked the ball into the bush we made sure we found it out even if it took us the reminder of the day.

Playing around and under the mango trees, we would fall down wittingly, pretending to have been injured at play. But we had our devoted eyes up at the ripe mangoes for late-night operations. We took turns in the survey and at different branch locations. Then we safeguarded the memory up to our hair follicles and impatiently waited for the fall of darkness. The moonlit nights were not friendly to our plots at all.

We played the trick so well that any teacher watching us for mischief would flinch and sympathize with us, thinking we were hurt. To their greatest surprise the ripen mangoes would be gone with us and digesting in our abdomens by daybreak, almost at the same time our teachers would be looking straight at our faces for signs of hidden guilt, but found none.

As young as we were, innocent as we looked, and as helpful as we were to everyone who needed our tender hands with lifting some pieces of firewood or calabashes of pond water onto his head, I look back at those days to think that we were as sneaky as the fox.

At that time also, instead of engaging in the monkey business as we did, we could have been more creative in our thoughts and industry if we had toys to play with and Ferris wheels to ride on.

We could have been Olympic swimmers if we had swimming pools to practice in and would have been great writers if we had libraries where we could have read the work of others.

There were times though, when luck ran out on us and we took our penalties. We were simply every day kids, who had to deal with the nuisance of growing up.

Spanking us in the general assembly for meddling with the school property was painful and humiliating, but it never stopped us from being boys—nothing ever seemed to slow us down. We had too many free hours to our advantage. After each day of school, the rest of the evenings became our managed property. We had no after-school programs, except at the time we became of age to attend catechism lessons for our first Holy Communion.

The first quarter of every year, during Easter break, when the mango trees were in full bloom with fruits, was the period when our school premises occupied our minds more than any other thing, even food or coca kola.

On weekdays we spent more daylight hours with our teachers than our parents. Therefore our teachers could guess our heights correctly in twilight and could tell how each of us walked and ran.

They had our names on top of their lips and could sing or whistle with them at any given opportunity. They also knew our fathers, especially mine because my dad was always in our school for children's immunizations.

For that reason we devised multiple strategies that helped us to escape in darkness without a trace. For example, we ran in directions completely different from the ways we came, so that the teachers would be thrown off that we were the culprits. They knew the villages we came from.

The trick worked, but put other innocent boys of our age and heights under suspicion and under constant surveillance. Instead of guilty feelings, we replaced our acts with the notion of cleverness. It was quite a game, which we won 98% of the time.

At one time or another one of us would assume the duty of a night guard, set with a catapult and solid pebbles to scare the snooping teachers away until we had our hands and pockets full.

Mangoes have very strong smell that easily gave us away. So we made sure we didn't put on the same pants until our moms washed them for us. Kids like us were not enthusiastic of bathing every day, but we would bathe to drive the mango smell into the unknown.

After each assault, we ate as many of the fruits as we could and buried whatever was left in the soil for fear of being queried and disciplined by our parents because home was equally as perilous as our school.

We were faced with two disciplinary fronts, none of which had less consequence. If, for example, my father or mother saw me with the mangoes, they would certainly tell on me.

Overall, we had immense delight, not only with our successes in plucking the mango fruits, oranges, and pineapples without being caught, but in our childish act of injecting fears into the jelly hearts of our teachers.

Between their front lawn and the soccer field was stationary darkness at night. Next to it was a bleeding graveyard, east of the school. Whereas the teachers feared to leave their houses at night, the darkness meant nothing to us.

Some teachers had flashlights that illuminated not more than two feet away. Maybe they bought only two batteries in a year and expected them to last forever. They were stingy to the core and obviously dedicated their flashlights for going to their pit toilets at nighttime.

All kinds of snakes and other animals fed fat in the teachers' outhouses and often we got news that teachers, their wives or children had snake bites at night, going to the bathroom, and were sent to the hospital.

Year after year, teachers narrated several folk stories that left the image of death in our minds, but we brushed them off as quickly as possible, before they had roots in us. Our intention was clear; if we feared the night, teachers would enjoy the fruits all by themselves and not a single day did they consider us having a bite of it.

Often they told us about the "three-headed-gliding-ghosts" that control the blankets of darkness. They also told us that darkness was evil and dangerous and asked us to avoid it. We glance at one another to steal a quick dumpy smile at the story we thought was meant to undermine our time table. Because of the syrupy of the delicious mangoes in our minds, some of us, nonbelievers, simply brushed off their terror stories.

We enjoyed tremendous freedom, void of the serious threats surrounding both the young and the old now at the mercy of kidnappers and the amount of ransom they demand.

Second is the scale of armed robbery. From the above perspective, I'm happy to recognize how good we were to quickly drop all the childish behaviors and not allow them to follow us to our adulthood.

In retrospect, we thought the ridiculous fairytales played out in our favor, we took advantage of the nights, big time.

There were no street lights at the time. Perhaps, the nearest street lights we even heard of were about nine hundred miles, away in Lagos, the Federal Capital of Nigeria and some part of Enugu, about 200 miles, the capital of East Central States then.

From time to time one of us would be down with fever, diarrhea, and dysentery. More often than not, we thought our bad health was some kind of divine whip for our mischief. As young kids, we ran away from medications as ice melts with heat. Childish as it was, some of us who were courageous would swallow our medicines in exchange of a piece of meat.

Being quick on our feet, we were able to escape from the teachers' punishments; but could not get away from the ill effects of our unhealthy eating habits. Whereas our feet and our night activities were under our control, our health must have been controlled by some other invisible forces that pitilessly held us down; run, we could not; eat, we could not play, we quit and moaned in pain.

Any rainy night was a good sign of a rich harvest, for we loved the rains as much as the aroma and sweetness of the mangoes and the pineapples. We contributed money to buy a penknife to peel the pineapple and then shared it among ourselves. I don't think we washed neither our hands nor the pineapples before we devoured them. Those habits comprised our problems.

Sometimes, when we were very sick for a day longer than we thought, we flashed on our religious doctrine, in which, we learned that the punishment for sin is death. To be spiritually cleansed, we argued and agreed that the fruit plucking didn't qualify for sin or for death. We quickly classified our deeds as ordinary pranks.

In some ways, we were bad. But to compare what we did, growing up, we were holy innocents. We never stole money from anyone, nor broke into people's houses.

As sweet and innocent as we were, compared to the present, we picked up lost monies and handed them over to our teachers when school was in session or to our parents, after school hours and during vacations, who then handed the money over to the church catechist for lost and found announcements.

These days, if you lose about anything, don't hope to get it back; things have changed to a large extent.

As kids, we did not have an idea of where any landmines of jeopardy were. Our Guardian Angels whom we constantly relied upon led us through to safety and we had a duty to thank them after it was all over; they did a good job.

Amuzi was one of the leading communities in church, school performances, soccer, and other outdoor entertainments. She shows off in the annual festival—the feast of Saint Jude, October 28. The Saint Jude's festivals are magnets to all the angels, the deaf, and the lame because of what it offers.

In the celebration of the feast, 1962, Amuzi made news when the female teens played soccer with men over sixty years of age and won them by the score of three goals to one (3-1 in favor of the ladies).

In another event, the more elderly men, about 80 years and above who fought the First World War, the second, and the intertribal wars of their time, were historic in demonstrating their old techniques in the battlefields. The demonstrations drew multitude of people comparable to the crowd seen in the American air and water shows of July 4, annually.

During the St Jude's annual festivity, Amuzi people offer free food, wine, and beer to their guests beyond anyone's imagination. They work for it, save for it and brag about it; free food and beer for all! You can't miss it. It's like all you can eat and drink.

Each household goes all-the-way to entertain the number of guests she has, starting from 10 a.m. to 7 p.m. luckily enough, it takes place at the end of the rainy season, and with bright skies and longer days than nights, people stop at nothing enjoying the festival as long as they want.

In 1971, one year after the civil war, of course the festival was not celebrated any time in the three year the war between Biafra and the rest of Nigeria. So the celebration of the festival in 1971 served as groundbreaking get together, a kind of reunion where we all gathered for merriment for the first time in three years without fear of looking up for the British and Israeli bombers fighting on the Nigerian side. We had a lot of joy and renewed spirit. We moved on as well as get along with everyone to put the past behind us.

To say the least, the people's bounteousness has earned Amuzi people many friends and that has as well influenced many young men and women from neighboring communities to incorporate their marriage preference toward Amuzi, in order to share excitedly in the annual tradition of the festival and the good will of the people.

You might think tradition and culture fade away with age, but here, people do a bundle to sustain what they have, especially if it serves their identity well.

In my recent observation I have witnessed how well-attended and largely organized the religious festival is today, after missing it for a long time. It is still significantly insulated, self-sufficient, and healthy.

My take-away from the experience doesn't need a psychic to interpret why the Amuzi girls are reluctant to leave for elsewhere to marry until they have religiously explored their chances of grasping a suitor from within Amuzi community. I truly love the tradition and wish there's a magic wand we could wave to help make them realize their dreams. I hope we can.

To further keep the culture alive and healthy, I think I would encourage every young girl to continue with the tradition of inter-village marriages than a distant one. I would as well suggest for them to include international citizens, who could assist in making their migration to any part of the world possible.

Commonly known, the Indians and the Mexicans in the United States marry within their race; that's why their population constantly punches the skies, while many Africans stay home and choose crime over creditable endeavors.

Chapter 4

The Hidden Why

Taking a look from the mid 70's to the late 80's, things have changed dramatically, from African emigrants not visiting home in decades to now the outburst of yearly summer and Christmas vacations, from letter writing to instant telephone calls, electronic mails, and to text messaging. Today, there is outburst of huge investments in ultramodern homes and shipment of automatic cars and trucks, like we have never seen before. Western Union transfers and Money Gram have created overwhelming false impression that America is a land of riches and deposits of hundred dollar bills for anyone to grab.

That impression has more than ever added to the craze and the expectation of not only Africans, but other third-world countries.

Behind the false perception about the American allegory unfortunately, there is ignorance of foreign exchange rate. Africans have little idea of how hard it is to earn a living here besides the paying of high cooling and heating bills. To own a home and pay for the mortgage, not including the frequent maintenance, are the lessons that not many of us have the time to explain to people in Africa.

Here is one of the problems: I heard from someone who bought an expensive wedding gown and a tree piece-suit for his wedding in Africa, just to show off. And two days after he returned, he said, he sent both the suit and wedding gown to the drycleaners, and then returned them to the stores where he bought them for full refund. A first impression matters, but a false impression is an express way to nowhere.

The situation about the foreign exchange rate might not make sense without telling the whole story.

In my early summer trips of 2004, a paternal second cousin's wife, Ann, came to me after a Sunday service and dynamically asked me to give her a dollar—one dollar ($1).

"Give you just a dollar?" I asked.

Without hesitation, she whizzed her tongue out in the air, face up, and both eyes lifted up to the sky, and swore earnestly how seriously she wanted to "touch and feel one American dollar."

I thought she would have asked for another, maybe a hundred dollar bill or a fifty, but she didn't. She certainly was unaware about exchange rates and that larger bills of fifties or hundreds are needed to have meaningful value: Be careful what you ask for, okay?

"Yes sir," she replied.

I was told later that she traveled to the state capital, Owerri about 20 miles away to exchange the single dollar bill for the local currency, Naira—(N).

I couldn't help, but pity the woman for spending her local currency in transportation, money she could have used for her needs.

To my guess, the round-trip fare might have cost her at least, N200 while the value of the single dollar bill that I gave her was, at the time, about N10 if she was lucky to find a buyer. The bad news is that the foreign exchange traders do not, I repeat, do not buy single dollar bill; they say it is not in demand at all. They would even give you a couple of single dollar bills free.

Therefore, it's more than likely, Ann, my paternal cousin's wife came back with the dollar, unsold. Did she get more than what she ever bargained for? I'll leave the rest of the story to anyone's guess.

Further to the psychic grip of the America's wealth in the minds of our families at home, many of us, with dual citizenship go home to add more gas to the open flame—leaving phony impressions of material comfort and a shower of irrelevant affluence, portraying that we soak ourselves in silver and liquid gold in America and go home to fly our kite in colors. This is wrong.

It's a pity the counterfeit impression we created in the minds of the people is backfiring. African-Americans have largely become the targets of armed robbers and kidnap-for-ransom. Some of the tribulations are planned by the immediate family members. Perhaps the visiting brothers entrusted the family members with building projects in Africa. Soon, the caretakers begin to live big and beyond their new income. They transform their lifestyles in readiness for chieftaincy installation.

When questions of mismanagement of funds arise, there are no answers. They want to make Santa Clause off you all the year round. You would be stupid if you didn't expect the unexpected. They want to continue exchanging dollar and spend it without a balance sheet. It's like don't ask, don't tell; how about that?

Here is my message. Hear it now, hear it all, and hear it from me: love your brothers, sisters and close relatives as much as you can. Give them money for their needs. Buy them microwaves and show them how to use them. Buy them freezers, generators, and refrigerators; help them in every way possible, but never, ever trust them with your projects that require records keeping and answerability.

Do not forget that they have lately grown so big with your money, grown disrespectful to their seniors and would at any slight provocation insult you for your money that elevated them to affluence.

They might have respected you in the past; they shred the respect and throw garbage into the ocean if you ask questions about the why of things, as record of spending. You will be disappointed how cold their lies would dwell upon you. You would be given manufactured catalog of unpaid bills for your projects and demand full payment before they could sit down with you for any dialogue which would be valueless anyway.

What else do you want to hear and how loud would you like my voice to be. Give your projects to contractors and kick them out for another if you find them dishonest. There will be no hostility beclouding your family and your pathways.

Our big homes are mere vanity boxes and I share in the blame for building one in Africa. I was ignorant about the size and cost. What happened is this: After giving a sketch of the features I needed in my house and negotiated with an architect, I returned to the U.S.

By the time I re-visited home, two years later, the construction had been carried out of proportion and it was too late for any meaningful economic amendment. My plan was to have a house of about 3,000 sq ft. but ended up with a total of 9,100sq.ft, nine bedrooms, one family room upstairs and two living rooms downstairs. It is ridiculous and irresponsible, especially when you don't live the house as large, but visit only once in 3 - 4 years apart. Such being the case, you've built the house for rats, lizards, roaches and spiders to occupy and when you open the doors thy come out in straight lines, look at you in the face and wonder why you disturb their peace.

Another blunder we fall prey is the rush back home for a "quid pro quo" traditional title.

For the records, traditional chieftaincy titles are and should be the ordination of resident individuals who have contributed to the development, peace, and wellbeing of their people. The contributions may not necessarily have been in cash, but in kind, transparency, in character, outspokenness, as well as leadership, and track-record of good judgments.

What chieftaincy titles used to be and the purposes they served are different from what they are today. The titles were based on merit, accompanied with vast honor and respect. Title holders contained the

complex characters and behaviors of the growing generation at the time federal, state, and local government administrations were too fare away and out of reach to distal communities. Law enforcement officers and court administrations were few and remotely located too. The chiefs were responsible for their constituencies' peace and harmony. They were heads of their community town hall meetings. They were their local ambassadors and advisers, accountable to an "Eze"—superintendent of the chiefs. They were levy collectors in their respective constituencies.

To explain, Ezes and chiefs were similar to the counselor members and local government chairpersons we have today. The chiefs had regular face-to-face meetings with the Ezes. They settled land disputes and petty family wrangles. They were also in charge of normal pathway repairs and local market maintenance.

They did good jobs when rural communities needed all hands on deck to guide the youth and they strictly warded off criminals through unwritten laws passed over from one generation to another. If one was caught stealing, he would be sent to "Egypt," whatever that means, a near guess would be sold in slavery.

All in all, through their transparent honesty, the traditional rulers were also their people's banks, and it was through them traditional marriages were arbitrated and tie together.

Through their chain of command from chiefs to Ezes, community and family lands and cash crops were shared in exclusive preference to the first sons of the family.

By the laws of the land first sons of every family are responsible for the burial expenses of their fathers. If their fathers died when they were not yet financially able to offset the cost of their father's burial, they would be excused from the financial responsibilities for the burial.

It is terribly unrealistic, for an absentee chief, to referee marriages, share community properties, collect local levies, and settle complex family feuds from places such as Asia, Europe, and North America to the remote villages in Africa.

There are also people back home in far-away cities that spend money to be conferred with traditional titles. I have personally nothing against these fellows—close relatives of mine: cherished friends, countrymen; in-laws, and cousins that I have great respect for. I am happy that some of the absentee title holders I have spoken to agree with me about how undeniable my facts about the growing trade in the traditional title deal are.

I have never considered my differences in opinion about philosophy, religion, politics, and culture as cause for loosing my friends, rather it is through my cordial relationship I trade my passion about what I believe and the things I don't.

Where I think we have a hitch is the business of influencing tradition in a negative light. We should not make any mistake about it—tradition is not practiced remotely, nor delegated. It is completely different from the technology of telephone, fax, electronic mail, and text messaging.

Observably, the rules have not been rephrased but, they have evidently been tilted through greed and material desire. That is why things are not all worth the same today and the center no longer holds.

We should preserve and celebrate culture and tradition as they have been and not as we deem fit.

Furthermore, the models of our cars may change from year to year; we may choose to wear our pants further down below our butts, tradition and culture exist without models. They can only be passed on from one generation to another—as is, without inducement and adulteration. As we struggle to save the earth, we should include the preservation tradition.

To be precise, I don't think anyone has problem with someone eating his French fries before his hamburgers or the other way round. We, however, do by all means think something is fundamentally wrong if we continue to force our personal interest over and above institutional norms, as in the case of one introducing himself as "Dr. High Chief, Xyz," "Prince Xyz," "Rev. Dr., Dr. Xyz," and "Very High Chief Abc." It is silly if we continue to destroy novelty.

I hear someone say if we don't see anything wrong with this format then a psychological evaluation is unconditionally mandatory.

Culture is similar to our social security numbers; we do not swap them. They are unique in values.

I have often had many Americans ask me to explain to them what it means for someone to be a prince or a chief.

Usually, I handle their questions by asking what they are told the prince or chief means. With a head start I would unveil the details. One of them, my manager, Tim Henderson, said he has heard some say their fathers own many oil farms, including gold and silver collieries.

My response generally is that if my father had that much wealth, I wouldn't be in America for any economic or social reason. And for those that claim they have gold and silver quarries, I told Tim to ask them why they don't dress in chains of silver and gold hanging from their necks down to their toes. If you've got it, don't say it, but show it! That's what I would do.

Then also I advised Mr. Tim I would ask such person for some free gifts of the gold and silver and, as a matter of fact, some monetary donation.

I don't think I have seen many resident Africans in the U.S. fly in the first class aircrafts. We're all squished in the popular economy class.

Again, anyone could raise his self-esteem in assorted ways, but doing so with tradition, is a reversal of social order. We may stylishly claim anything without grating institutional values.

With the exception of the mess in tradition, how would anyone not like Africans overseas? The men are handsome, stylish dashing, and hardworking. The majority of them are well groomed, with clean shaving and put on terrific cologne.

They are comfortable in themselves. "To see them keep their shoulders high and walk as though the world belongs to them alone is fascinating," an African grand mother said.

Their women have two wardrobes layered with basic attires and each in spruce of recreating traditional outfits that are inestimably stylish, graceful, and beautiful looking. Their body language tells it all; self assuring, happy, smart, and knowledgeable icons.

If you don't know what a good cook these women are, try attending their parties or their naming ceremonies. Afterwards, you would need to signup for a 24-hour fitness to deal with the extra weight you've added due to their sumptuous free lunch or dinner.

As unique as the women are, they spray sweet fragrances in their bathroom cabinets and wardrobes with myrrh, aloes, and cinnamon.

The men make them feel good about themselves; they have different ways they storm their enthusiasm without overstating, "I love you."

If by an act of God the word—love slips off the men's mouth, it would be preserve it as long as it takes.

In this day and age where people change partners like outfits, African wives hold onto their men, as their men hold solid unto them.

The women are so good at whatever they're doing and that's why the men can't keep their hands off them.

Let us therefore leave some local tradition alone and be fluid in what we are doing best. Let us not wreck history so history will not wreck us.

Going home to throw a lavishing party to the people is tastefully a subculture, good enough to feed a people that are pathetically undernourished. But placing a flag of tradition attainment behind it is not in any way the best method to show off eminence.

I think it's time for us to sit back and access what we are doing wrong and what we need to do legitimately.

One quick fix, though, is that if we don't want to be continuous victims of the infinite serious crimes in our environment every one of us should desist from visiting home in Africa until things change a bit.

It does not matter how many excess luggage we carry in the airplane to benefit our extended families, there are yet so much to be done to improve the lives of the people, but we can only do so much; progress is scuffle by lawlessness and greed.

Those of us who own houses in Africa have our homes burglarized by the same people you help.

Today Africans are more materialist than ever before and the catch is that they don't want to work for it.

School children want mobile phones at all cost. They steal them from individuals and from the retailers and if they can't steal them, they go out begging for them.

You cannot estimate the percentage of unemployment in Africa for lack of reliable records.

Currently, the four major industries for students and applicants in Africa are: Canopy telephone offices, where the owners retail telephone call-cards; Okada—motorbike transportation, armed robbery, and kidnapping for ransom.

The "Okada transportation," is a storm of commercial motorcycles intensely penetrating public roads without any regard for traffic regulations. Among the operators, about 95% of them neither have licenses nor insurance coverage required by law to operate the motor vehicles. If they have licenses and insurance they are more than likely counterfeited somewhere around the corner at about 90% less than the price of the genuine papers.

Nevertheless, the police officers who are assigned to check crimes go out there, each for his daily financial benefit.

It doesn't matter whether the road users have genuine documentation or not, of course the police have no formal training in identifying which document is genuine and which one is not one. They would stop any motorcycle operator for bribe, not for insurance or motor license infractions.

They don't care a dime. One might even be in trouble showing the police a genuine document because they don't get anything out of you if you are lawful. You would be calling for a fight if you are genuine. "Oga, nor bi de thin we go chop, o! We go-go office." That's what you'll hear from the police. If you get there, you are finished!

A fraudulent government turns out corrupt society, it isn't concerned about the fate of the common man on the street.

An example of the level of corruption is the case in which the inspector General of a Police (IGP) who was convicted of embezzling about 20 billion naira of police fund.

Criminals caught by the civilian security are handed over to the police department and in a couple of hours or days the police accepts bribe from them and set them free without court action.

In 2008 a Judge from the River State of Nigeria told me that the police department has stripped them of their official duties. According to her, "the police carry out their enforcement duties and turn around to be proctors, judges, and cashiers without government records and receipts."

A blogs off the Internet, titled "Nigerian Police And Corruption," January 11, 2006, reads:

"Hey whats up y'all Nigerians? I feel that our police is corrupt - even P Square in oga police said that na wetin you go do for this life wey police no go come harrass you but I personally think that our police can't be faulted completely. I mean, the federal government doesn't pay them well and that's why they extort money. I mean should they die? How will they? And us Nigerians take them as mere human beings and we use them to show off like bodyguards and stuff."

January 13, 2006, 08:44 PM "our police are not corrupt. Our police are corruption itself!"

January 14, 2006, 06:01 PM

"Because the don't get enough money 2 feed their family, so they rather go 4 bribe"

Nigeria is in trouble and she needs help from within and outside of the country.

The most devastating organized crime that has stood firm is the kidnap-for-ransom. Again, the ill-equipped police have little idea on how to offset the crime.

It's spectacular to see the police pull off their federal uniforms at the whistle of automatic raffles.

The difference is, here, in America our police do not run away from criminals, they go after them. Also if we have a moving violation or fail to renew our motor vehicle license and insurance we settle it in traffic court, not with the police officer.

Fighting it out: Militants say they have been left out of talks on the Delta's future.

Over 10,000 barrels of highly flammable oil were spilt in the nine states that make up the Niger Delta news.bbc.co.uk/.../html/7.stm

Thursday, 5 July 2007, 23:42 GMT 00:42 UK

"Three-year-old seized in Nigeria

"The three-year-old daughter of a British expatriate worker has been kidnapped by gunmen in the Niger Delta, Nigerian police have said."

The child, Margaret Hill, was seized from a car on her way to school in the oil city of Port Harcourt.

According to the news, the kidnapping followed the case of five oil workers on Wednesday, July 4, 2007 the first since the main militant group in that area called off a month long ceasefire. The UK's Foreign Office called for the "immediate safe release" of the girl.

A spokesman said: "We do not know who took her. We are in contact with her parents and are providing assistance. High Commission officials are in contact with the Nigerian authorities."

When foreign workers in the Niger Delta were taken hostage, the rest of country did nothing but watch. The government of Nigeria did very little to stop the militants' increasing criminal acts. Then when the foreign contractors left and the militant's source of income by ransom was shut down their game changed; they turned their guns to the citizens of their own country.

The BBC's correspondent, Alex Last, in Lagos, said that in almost all previous cases it is foreign oil workers who have been taken hostage but in recent months the children of wealthy Nigerians have also become targets. I lived in the heart of the Niger Delta for nine months and I saw the lives destroyed beyond preservation. There are no good roads and the existing roads have no drainage to ward off mixed flooding of oil and rain. I saw primary schools and high schools in the most awful conditions, unworthy of occupancy. When it rained a mixture of oil and water flooded the schools. As a result, students stayed home and lost many hours of their instructions to the equatorial rains and terrible governance.

A Nation in trouble: Who would doubt that rebellion is not the product of procrastination and that it's when we are not involved in our communities with social problems, no matter how minute, we endure the lasting consequences that are associated with our carelessness and delays?

It doesn't matter how proficiently situated a journalist might be, describing the horrific situation and suffering of our brothers and sisters in the Niger delta communities does not tell the whole stories of the suffering group of people.

Without laying the foundation of who they were as a peace-loving people before they got where they are now, without the statistics on the fertility of their lands, their agricultural industry and the produce of the people before the oil pollution turned it into rubbles and waste lands, any account about the Niger Delta would be muddled and fundamentally incomplete.

Before all eyes turned on the delta region, the waterways of the Niger Delta were major outlets to the Atlantic. Much seafood, fresh and dry, came from there. The delta region was a land rich in cassava, yam, and cocoyam tubers; out-of-season vegetables and corn were abundant.

It also used to be home for cash crops such as palm oil and nuts, mangoes, cocoanuts, and oil beans, bananas, plantains, pineapples, including raffia palm, from which innovative alcohols were extracted.

Other neighboring regions depended on the rich lands of the delta for their food supplies. Places like Etchee, Orishieze, and other suburbs accommodated energetic young men by hiring them to work on their farms.

Many people whom I knew relocated to these areas lived there permanently, married, raised their children, and educated them through their earnings from the farms. They came home only when they became too old and weak to labor in the farms.

In the months I lived within the creeks and the tributaries of the Niger Delta with the people, I exchanged views with them, bought my needs from the same market as they did, and of course, experienced the mosquito bites and the persistent rain fall that characterized the equatorial zone in Africa.

After every rain, I saw flood mixed with crude oil floating and sparkling like a liquid mirror. Through the reflection I could see the clouds, the sun, the moon, and the stars below my feet.

Flood of oil in water that meandered through the footpaths, motorways, homes, and had their resting places in schools, soccer fields, in the market places and church premises.

With the topography of the delta barely above the sea level, I could not find a higher ground to stay in case the situation of flooding went off hand. I lived in the polluted waters.

I chose to live on the ground floor of the hotels for fear that the houses might collapse with the increased precipitation and flooding. Seeing the haphazardness of things on the bare surface, I was doubtful of the strength of the foundation of the houses. They might have been built on shallow and spongy soil. I always parked away from the houses so that my car would be safe if any of the walls collapsed, and if I was lucky to make it alive I could still have my car to go back home.

From the worn-out look of things and how unsupervised I thought things were, I was convinced the houses might have been built without a touch and direction of structural engineers.

If things were a little organized, if the people were given opportunities for good education and employment, if the villages and market places were set up with government-approved plans, and piles of garbage all over the place carted away to landfills, and if there were gutters and drainages, life would have been a celebration in the River State rather than a condemnation. Homes, schools, churches, roadways, and market infrastructures would not be sunk and dripping in the flood of crude oil and the rains. It is unsightly and unhealthy. It is evil. It's a rape of luck.

Instead of a fine polish of wealth and glories of oil fields, I saw graveyards of people all over the towns and villages—men, women and children, who either perished as a result environmental pollution or were killed in the course of fighting for their human rights. The dead are buried in the front view of the compounds, which embitters the families and make them take up arms for lawlessness and revenge. To think of the innocent black and beautiful lives that have been wasted in these areas gives me nightmare.

These are people, who through no choice of theirs were born in a place to live to their full potentials and to contribute their fair share to national building, but have been dehumanized and demonized by the system. The emergent situation is reminiscent of the plague by the so-called oil curse—an economic syndrome known as Dutch disease, which was named after the troubles that weighed down the Netherlands in the 1960s.

I wonder when the civil society is going to stop turning their ears, eyes, and minds away from the region. I believe there are things we can do. I believe we can all with one voice say enough is enough.

To France, Germany, England, and United States of America, I say to you: You have for decades enjoyed the natural resources of the region in peril of extinction; a lot of the wealth from the oil money is in your national banks and a lot of property has been bought in your countries from the oil revenue out of the same region; now is the payback time. Come help those who need your help.

We all know that if the outside world throws in some lifejackets there will be hope for the region. We all know that with their help, especially the United States, respected and honored for her selfless growth and expansion of good will, things will normalize, and lives will be saved. Don't send money; I entreat you, send a study group for assessment and recommendation of a way forward. Save your relief, but send for the president and his cabinet for some form of orientation to avoid total collapse of law and order.

Would anyone like to change shoes with the delta communities? Let us assume that these people are our biological parents, brothers, sisters, sons and daughters. How would anyone feel if his family was in this ruthless condition? Do we forget or pretend not to know that what goes around comes around? Instead of war, can't we let peace reign? War is cold-blooded, while doing acts of kindness to someone unleashes acts of love, which is a natural gift of fullness and reward.

My nine months of experience living within the people and communities exposed a whole lot of issues, which an outsider like me could not have known, ever.

My hotels in Ahoda were Sam Royal and Group Girl. Through their glass windows I could see both poverty and hopelessness on the faces of young boys and girls, whose lives have been dampened because of the poor foundation of their schools and education.

Through fumes from standby power generators I could see frustration in their faces and in my interviews with some of them they made roll calls of how their fathers, brothers, and cousins have gone through protests against the abject neglect of their people and suffered negative responses and punishments.

In Borie, Ogoni, and Eleme, I saw pervasive sexual abuse of girls from 13-16 years of age by the so-called "oil men" – oil workers from foreign and local companies – who voraciously took advantage of poor, unprotected, innocent children, and did so with impunity. When the teenage girls became pregnant the men abandoned them in the same manner the federal government has abandoned the communities—a place where law and order should have been the main concern of the government to protect its major source of foreign exchange earnings.

The extent to which groups have poisoned the Delta Region has not been largely reported. Analysis in the journal of African Affairs 100:27-54 (2001) suggests the state and corporate response to the Niger Delta crisis has so far been inadequate in the sense that it fails to satisfy the demands of the local people. The article title Corporate and state responses to anti-oil protests in the Niger Delta stated:

"Judging from past experience, unless there are structural changes within Nigeria's institutional framework, which would allow for a more effective use of the country's oil wealth for the benefit of the oil-producing areas, conflicts in the Niger Delta are likely to continue."

In the News release, Friday 16th March 2001—Woodside take-over: Nigerian refugee tells "Shell's domination of industry, puppeteering of govt, rampant pollution, political murders."

"Today Friends of the Earth, Sydney released a statement from a political refugee "Mary" who has fled oppression by the Shell military-industrial complex in Nigeria. Mary's statement identifies Shell as a corporate criminal involved in massive destruction of farmland in her homeland in the Niger Delta by way of oil pollution. Mary tells of Shell's funding and supply of weapons to the puppet Nigerian government. Mary tells of Shell's complicity in the murder of subsistence farmers and political opponents of the oil pollution." *www.sydneyalternativemedia.com/id147.html*

In March, 1999 the U.S. congressman, Dennis J. Kucinich and several members of congress called for congressional investigation in the killing of civilians, human rights abuse and the reason Chevron used Nigerian security forces against the oil producing delta region in Nigeria.

The human rights group filled a suit against Chevron in the U.S. for perpetuating human rights abuses of cruelty, inhuman treatment and, cruelty, violation of rights to life, liberty, and security peaceful assembly, wrongful death, and unfair business practice in the region.

When Saro-Wiwa, a social and environmental activist in Rivers state and others were arrested for trial, a leading British counsel, Michael Birnbaum QC, writing about his experience in the case of Saro-Wiwa's stated: "It is my view that the breaches of fundamental rights are so serious as to arouse grave concern that any trial before this tribunal will be fundamentally flawed and unfair."

It was exposed Shell and Texaco oil companies were in collaborations with Chevron in their do-or-die policy against the peaceful delta activists.

In November 10 1995 Saro-Wiwa and eight others were executed against international appeals for leniency. The execution drew international condemnation and outrage against both the military junta and Shell.

(http://news.bbc.co.uk/2/shared/spl/hi/picture_gallery/04/africa_polluting_nigeria/html/1.stm)

The former Prime Minister of United Kingdom, Sir John Major, 1990 to 1997, described the trial as "a fraudulent trial, a bad verdict, an unjust sentence. It has now been followed by judicial murder."

http://www.remembersarowiwa.com/pdfs/Life_death_KSW.

It is troubling in the ways foreign oil companies are superseding the law in their favor, bribing and waging wars against the people they do business in their lands, acts and violations that would send them to prison in the United States and England.

Another concern following the oil companies' scuffle within the delta, my interviewees in big cities of Abuja, Lagos, Onitsha, and Kaduna said some politicians engage in mobilizing gangsters for the purpose of winning elections. "The use of militants during elections is as old as Nigerian elections itself and the federal and state elections of 1999 legitimized it," one of my interviewees stated. He went further to affirm that after the elections, thugs formed cult groups each trying to assert vast authority and superiority over the other. The supremacy tussle, he added, has claimed a lot of innocent lives as the cult groups are used to silence opponents as police stood on the sidelines.

Asking a couple of police officers why they have not been able to nip the problems in the bud, they said that things took a different dimension in 2007, when the chief financiers of the gangs lost grip of power after the elections and could no longer dictate the tune for the pipers—cultists.

According to them, when nothing positive was coming out of the commotion, the embittered politicians stopped funding their henchmen, so they resorted to kidnapping foreign oilmen for their continued means of their livelihood. They also stated that foreign oil companies were forced to withdraw their workers when they could no longer risk the lives in addition to the exorbitant ransom demanded by the kidnappers.

Consequently, they added, when the foreign oil workers left, many Nigerians—the upper-and middle-class-citizens suddenly became their new brand targets of abduction, which they emphasized has risen to be out of control, affecting every facet of the society.

Gangsterism is an act of brutality, comparable to huge machinery that no person knows how to operate, and when it gets out of control, it ends up tearing down the cause we thought we were fighting—the liquid gold we considered to be everything—riches. Unfortunately, it does look to me that Africa is running out of time.

Chapter 5

Blessed are the Peacemakers

In my many years of traveling to Europe and Asia, and having lived in Africa and America, I have never seen a nation as caring and compassionate as the American nation. We Americans go all out to save people trapped in ice while skiing on the mountains. We dive down the bottom of the ocean looking for people that have drowned, just to recover their bodies. The animal protection agency steps in to fight man's cruelty to animals. We even build shelter for strayed dogs and cats and give them up for adoption, but in two-thirds of the world, dogs are reared for their meat and beaten for their bad behavior.

We Americans have special places for children's protection. In airports, men and women traveling with their kids are given special privileges to board before others, while in other countries the culture is different.

In American hospitals and in doctors' offices, we do our best to help children and stop them from crying. We give them their favorite lollipops to show them that we care and love them. Health care for the children is top on our agenda.

At the entrance of our churches, movie theaters, restaurants, and day-care centers, we adults hold the doors for children and their parents to go in before us. At schools, the heat of summer and in the freezing cold of winter, teachers and principals stand as long as it takes to watch for the safety of children as they are dropped off in the morning and picked up in the afternoon. At any given time in any given place, Americans are the first to rush overwhelming aid of food and medicine to places and countries at war or those struck by natural disaster. We spend billions in aid to Africa against the spread of AIDS and HIV. These are praiseworthy programs, which other nations might be doing, but not as much as the U.S.

In his inaugural address to Americans and the world, President Barack Obama said: "Is there anyone out there, who still doubts that America is a place where all things are possible."

I share in the philosophy about everything being possible in America with a little bit of modification: An appeal that will include just one thing in our ability to leading the world in problem-solving. And that speaks to our blueprint of giving aid to Africa that has not yielded much of the expected result so far. To ease the third world's most endemic problems, we should consider giving them quarterly workshops on national building and accountability.

Secondly, seeing that we are known to be the most generous nation on earth, we should not look away or pretend not to know that about three-quarters of African nations' looted treasury, especially from Nigeria, is harbored overseas. Much of the loot has also been converted to real estate and personal business investments.

Having proclaimed these facts in a nutshell, would anyone still wonder why the looted countries have no good roads, no pipe-borne water and why they are in this 21st century swaddled in darkness, without functional electricity and without industrialization? The hospitals, schools, and universities are in ruins, crime is uncontrollable. The statistics of unemployment is the highest ever recorded in history; yet Nigeria is about the fourth largest exporter of crude oil to the world market.

Is it out of place for anyone to question where the wealth of the nation is draining and who is draining it? How much longer would we be shying away from helping the nation to do what is right before it crashes into an all-out war? Isn't it better to do something now before we start seeing huge airplanes of International Red Cross and the World Council of Churches flying overheads dropping food and medicine for the displaced, the hungry, and the wounded?

I think more than ever, all eyes of humans, young and old across the continents are all over the U.S. to act and act now to save the situation. Let's help not only Nigerians, but other nations to retrieve and repossess her looted treasury. I believe we can and the time to act is now as the clock ticks to our hearing.

The challenge to take the bull by the horns, one that can spark a new form of care and aid, simply lies in the hands of one unique nation with its exclusive people. That nation is no other than the United States of America, born with the history of care not just for its people, but also for the tyrannized nations around the globe.

Crime is everywhere you turn the corner. Being critical about one crime and having a blind eye on another is as cruel as it its denial.

Research indicates that foreign banks in England, France, Belgium, Switzerland and, most of all, the United States, have aided and abetted the corruption that has crippled third-world countries for decades. I thought what is generally held as the rule of the thumb applies to one and all, not some.

Here is yet another challenge facing America in her will to reform the world to a more peaceful and generous state. It is out in the open who the foreign looters of their government treasuries are and where they unload their loot. We do know as well that unless the United States takes the lead in cracking them down no them, no other country will.

There have been few cases where government officials, mainly state governors or their agents trapped at some airports with millions of dollars and pounds to be kept in their foreign banks. Foreign security agents need to do more, and banks that have already received such huge deposits should find a way to repatriating the loot. It's just civil to do so.

Let us lead the way rather than look away. We shouldn't presume that a wildfire in a distant land has nothing to do with our own lands; it spreads. Helping to put out the wildfire of corruption is one of the most precious humanitarian aids to our credit without firing a shot of gun.

To harbor the bad guys is ethically wrong and religiously sinful. If thieves have nowhere to hide their stolen wealth they would stop stealing and find something else to do something legally recognized for national building.

What is surprising is that at the exit points of the international airports, you'll see the exchange-control officers standing tall, tough, and tight in their faces as combatant soldiers seriously demanding a declaration of liquid cash from travelers. By law of the United States of America you are allowed to carry the sum of not more than $10,000. A penny or more above it needs extra declaration and documentation.

While in the same airport, at the arrival points, the same control unit would be flashing their welcoming smiles, purposefully presenting a laidback attitude and worrying less about tens of thousands of dollars one is bringing into the country.

There is neither signal nor alarm for a person tiptoeing out of his country carrying in raw cash millions of pounds or dollars to put in a foreign account or to purchase property.

We see less commitment in stripping people down to their feet in search of excess cash. They do strip you down for drugs that tear down U.S. neighborhoods. Banks do the same thing with cash, not being rigid on their regulation of huge foreign customers' deposits and their sources. But you are not allowed to withdraw more than $10,000 without paper trail documentation.

Resolutely we ignore the arithmetic of matching the information in the foreign exchange declaration form with whatever cash the individuals bring into our country. It makes no sense; it's a double standard, and by application as well as by implication, robbing Peter to pay Paul.

The New York Times, Tuesday, February 17, 2009, write that Aliyu Mohammed, the Nigerian national security adviser, was scheduled to arrive in Washington that week to continue efforts to track down the money that was siphoned from Government treasuries by successive military and civilian leaders.

We all know very well who the corrupt officials and agents are what countries they come out of, but the thing that surprises everyone is the open arms in which we, Americans, the British, the French,

Germany, and all other developed nations welcome the looters, and their loot. The quickness in which their children's visas and admissions into schools and colleges are processed also send clear signals of aiding and abetting criminals. Whereas the children of ordinary people, struggling every day have their student visa applications and college admissions put under the shelf, abandoned, and discarded. How unfair that is!

Our world is in difficulty because it has chosen a reform without taking into account the basic operations of odd and Even number models. For example: if we add-up two odd numbers, our answer is an even number. On the other hand, if we subtract an even number from an odd number, we are left with an odd number.

It is very likely the public does not know all of the facts. Therefore, we need extraordinary media coverage to provide detailed accounts of the crises before we go to the next stage of problem-solving. If it looks like money laundering or looks like a duck and also swims like a duck it should get our attention.

There is no global furnace more ferocious and more inhuman than the prowling of one nation and piling the loot into the Banks of another nation.

Help! Help! Africans' eyes look on us for help and that big hope and help can only come from America. Africa knows that America cares and can help, if it wants. Africa has seen it through Oprah Winfrey and her celebrated school in South Africa to educate and empower young girls. Help now; Africa has no shelter for economic and social misfortune in form of food stamps. Help is Africa's last hope and help is the answer to its problems; not necessarily in form of cash.

The landing of a US Airways jet into the Hudson River in New York, January 16, in which all 155 passengers and their crew escaped alive, couldn't have been possible anywhere in Africa. The passengers would all be dead and their requiems long sang and over. African's ill-equipped divers, if ever they could be found, would hunt for cash and jewels of the dead. Their ill-gotten means is everything they care about.

Maybe only 5% of Africans have well-equipped national guards for emergencies. In Africa very few companies have health insurance for the sick. If there's drug-manufacturing company in Africa it may not be more than a dozen. Has anyone seen a made-in African car? Help, help, dire conditions need patriotic people.

We can help change the culture; help build national awareness so that the wildfire could be extinguished before it engulfs the rest of the generation. If problems of such magnitude don't qualify more than the so-called global warming and doesn't capture global attention, you be the best judge to tell what else should.

When social, traditional or cultural issues arise in a given place, cities, towns, and villages, we need not look away neither ignore it, nor wait for too long, or panic. Such situation need our inputs before they get out of hand or better.

There's nothing wrong in having different points of views and being in harmony at the same time with one another. What matters most is the respect we have for all—the young respecting their seniors and the seniors in turn should, as a golden rule, respect the juniors. If we fail to bring the value of respect to the front burner, we might get too far in facing up to the challenge of our time.

In the memo that I presented to a section of my community in the United States of America two days after I returned from my extended visit to Africa, Wednesday, December 22, 2004; I said that a responsibility to teach our people new acts of living, love, and care had emerged. Crises, many observers said to me, "We can't fix." And they were right, because of the various reasons that I tripped upon in my fact-finding mission.

In my presentation, I declared many of us were aware of the extreme hate and bitterness that plagued our people at home for some years now. The hostility as I learned came from an immaterial argument about the order of descendants and superiority among our four kinfolks.

For readability and understanding, I would illustrate the makeup of the rural neighborhood using the four chambers of the heart: First, the left and right atria, and second, the left and right ventricles.

What caused the seizure and a breakdown of law and order in the community is that the Right Ventricle bragged that it is the first descendant of the chamber and claims it has the final say in whatever happens within the chamber, whether the decisions were right or wrong.

The Left Ventricle felt the allegation was deliberate, insulting, and hateful and so called for local ruling to attest to the order of their offspring. The case about who was the first male descendant in the heart chamber involved other communities. Although the two upper chambers: the left and the right atria knew the answer, they stayed on the sidelines to watch the claim and counterclaims spiral until they were asked to testify.

Funny to mention, the trouble was brewing among people, who have neither single asset of land to share, no livestock, nor farm produce, nor any airplane landing and parking revenue to split; no social security savings, nor health insurance behind them.

Without a second thought, I took about two weeks to conduct interviews with 14 different families across the board. During the process, I noted some concealed support of the rift from some of us living in the U.S. This support did not help develop a clear-cut solution to the misunderstanding within our people inside and outside the community.

There wasn't a day or a time in my dreams that I could have thought that a people, pacesetters—so parented, educated, fervently religious with unparalleled exposures, could fall for such a diminutive fight as to be laughed at by other villagers and neighboring communities.

With all the data and confessions in my hand, I challenged every one of us, affirming that we were playing a hide-and-seek game over the serious matter and that we should understood the huge mistakes we were making. I thought it was worth our while to ask the pertinent questions about the causes and effects, and asked if we did not yet have a thoughtful move toward peaceful concessions and reconciliation. I maintained, it would mean nothing, but a victory over our strength.

I didn't want to be a lonely voice in a classic community matter that required community effort to deal with the disgrace that might diminish our legacy like the wax drips off the candle stick. So I called for help, listened to signs and voices of assistance, and patiently waited for help, hoping the visual narrative of what I saw and heard would melt the ice and ignite some concerns and compassion. I watched!

I perceived our people were bleeding and therefore demanded we examined our consciences for guilt of not encouraging the town criers and frantic whistleblowers to straighten out the rebellious subjects, who have abused the spotless values that have held the pe together all these years.

Notably, my target audiences were not moved, the ice in their hearts did not melt. They pretended not to recognize that the virtual bleeding I referred to was both internal and on the external demeanor of our kinfolks at home.

There was whispering and some of my addressees were desperate to know what I knew and from whom. I made it known the embarrassing effects the crisis at home was having on the people. In particular, the women told me they were fed up with how the men were leading them, and therefore, secretly admired my intervention.

I insisted we in the United States could help and believed I was making an urgent call ahead of time before anything got out of hand.

That help, I emphasized, would be on the way if we dug up the dirt that was leading our proud community in the wrong direction, a direction that had already walked its way into their wide-range devotions and practices, in the church, town-hall meetings, and in the funeral attendance of Pa Nicholas who was about 120 years, the oldest in town then.

The effect of the grudge also spun up to marriage celebrations that I witnessed, including the silver jubilee celebrations of Sr. Maria and Rev. Sebastian.

For all that mess, I demanded an answer by asking how serious could it get before we stood up for action.

I conveyed the words of the U.S. Secretary of State, Hillary Clinton, who wrote the book: "It Takes a Village." It would take all of us to act.

Subsequently, I expressed it won't take one person alone but all of us to extinguish the flame that has continued to burn in the hearts and minds of the people out of the worthless claim about "who is and who should be the head of the kindred." We would not be strangers in our community nor should we toss problems to a corner.

During my facts-finding visit, I knocked on doors and went into the people's huts and houses, and thought it was profane not to wish them good health, long lives, and extended happiness. I saw their dehydrated and distressed faces that spoke a thousand words and couldn't just hate any of them. I exchanged greetings with them; they never varied their looks or voices at me. I attended their weekly town hall meetings; it was by far less exciting and less productive than what it used to be when we were growing up.

I observed the attendance of the gathering; it was scanty and one-sided. The voices that I heard in their deliberations spat out nails and toxins. At that moment I said to myself, "God, is this home and are these people the same people, my people that I left a decade and half ago?"

A water-supply line going to one arm of the kindred blocked with concrete and cements mix was reason for the bitterness. I was told they had not paid their dues.

Looking for help to stop the bleeding I received cold reaction. In my view, I thought it was more honorable to install a filter in the water system than re-enforce pipelines of bitterness among them. That's not how we grew up. That's not how our parents trained us. I as well elaborated on how we could make our people benefit from our western exposure and experience, to provide valuable things, not just for the present but also for the next generation in mind.

I share in the school of thought that "a stitch in time saves nine," we have to start mending fences as disagreements arise. This will create a more conducive atmosphere for the next generation to build on.

Tearfully, I saw that the kids had been beaten hollow with the situation and so wore looks of helplessness. I sensed they needed sturdy and scrupulous voice to lighten them up.

In the words of Senator Robert F. Kennedy, "Children are the touchstone of value, and all society, all groups, and states, exist for their benefit."

I stated my stand for peaceful coexistence, no matter who was caught up in the gaffe. By this, I thought I had a home run for immediate discussion but was disappointed.

Guess what? My target audience had my email and only three, out of about sixteen got back with me. Only one of them sent me a written reply, which reads:

> "Dear Mel,
> Compliments of the season, to you and your family. Welcome back and thank you for the serious observations that you made. I is really shameful that with the death of your father, my father, Paul Emechete, Mr. Boniface Igbokwe, and others the peace makers are dead. If these individuals could hold the community together I wonder why we can't with all our education and wits. I hope that you realize that there is no longer Umuofor family meeting because they are trying to determine who is the head kindred. Amuzi is no better. I agree with you that we have to take the bull by the horn and put our head together and see what we can do. At least we can go to bed and say we have played our part. It has to start somewhere. Sadly it is not something that we can do from a distance. We have to be there to seek the solution. What bothers me is when the parish priests start taking part in politics. It is very dangerous for our people. Sometime we shall discuss in detail and see where we can start. We can also see those among us who will throw their supports aside and face the truth. We have to start at home first. Charity begins at home. Thanks for your concern and I have always been gravely concerned about the state of things at home. (Peter)."

This letter was written by a man disclosing genuine facts, while others just sat back without a word of contribution.

To sit back with out a word in a situation like this is the same as doing nothing if we had a fire that needed to be put out.

Soon after, other social problems began to spread, involving the larger community. Although the most revealing and spiteful reaction one ever thought of was the cold silence to such an important issue.

In a logical sense, you really begin to wonder if some of us are made of plastic, which brings to reference the Biblical teaching, asking: "If salt looses its flavor, where else shall it be salted?"

In practical terms, we know that if one is not part of a solution, he's certainly part of the problem. The silence of the people was a good indication that I hit the nail on the head.

A traveler, my father used to say, encompasses more experience than his counterpart in grey hair.

The more we travel, it becomes a lot easier for us to be enriched with facts rather than fiction, having deep, and physical touch of the world from the inside out. "We are judged by what we build, not by what we destroy," President Obama said. And to add to his voice, I believe silence to problems is as destructive as bad judgments.

We should be living in the new millennium of light and accommodation of one another in order to water the trees that we crave to grow and bear fruits. Unfortunately, the ripples of nonparticipation in community organizations do not waste time in reproducing organized crime, armed robbery and abduction- for-ransom—our greatest concern today. Charles Kettering, the inventor of the self-starting automobile, said that the only time we can't afford to fail is the last time we tried.

Chapter 6

The America Wonder

Among the many concerts we watched or acted in our primary school the one each of us still remember today is "American Wonder" and the songs that followed:

> America, America wonder, America, America wonder,
> America, America wonder, America, America wonder.

Second song was:

> Oh Mississippi, oh Mississippi,
> Mississippi carried my heart away
> Oh Mississippi, oh Mississippi
> Mississippi carried my love away.

At the end of the concert, it was everyone's piece of music.

Certainly this helped to shape our dreams about America and we all wanted to be here.

There's no telling how the third-world countries came to the concept that America is some kind of exclusive planet—a land of instant gratification where things happen without sweat.

Could it be as a result of American rich movies, our arts and culture, the many beautiful photographs of American cities, our roads, bridges, or the elegance of American lifestyle, especially of our celebrities?—American pride.

The news and the stories Africans hear about Oprah Winfrey long before she built a school in South Africa, blew their minds away. They don't know if Oprah is the richest woman in the world, what they admire is that Oprah is a woman and a black who is loving and kind.

Because of her humanitarian work they see her as a black angel – a type of angel they have never seen before.

Believe it or not in Washington, DC., two years ago a young man from Africa knelt down on arrival at the international airport and kissed the U.S. soil to glorify the nation and its worth.

Some Africans think America is not part of the earth, but some kind of a place in a mystery land, where no evil exists, no suffering is endured. To them everything made in America is packaged in a wonderland.

One specific example is this: When my parents-in-law visited us for the first time in South Holland, Chicago Illinois and saw me taking care of my vegetable garden, that was rich with tomatoes, okra, and green amaranth, my mother in law was surprised and said, "Oh, I didn't know America had land for garden."

And I replied, "Mom, you must be kidding me, what do you think we eat, if we don't?" She smiled and said it's because of the stories she heard about how differently America is—God's own country, with our food and water made and dropped down from heaven.

The people, our people, who exaggerate the American image, you will be surprised, might not have visited their state capital, ever. They watch CNN more than many Americans. They believe all crimes can be solved and that America is second to heaven. Sometimes it looks that way to me, no doubt, seeing how other nations are in regard to law and order.

Because America has countless number of blessings, if anyone told Africans we have incredible number of homeless people, they would think that you lied.

Despite America's economic troubles the election of President Barack Obama has drawn up more interest and attention, from old and young and has increased the number of American television viewers.

Again, with about 75 % unemployed, Africa has more time for TV, not all TV, but American television.

The third-world folks, who do not pay rents, living in their country homes and huts, many of them without good drinking water and electricity, might doubt the statistics of Americans who live on the streets. The extended-family practice in Africa on the other hand helps to make homelessness less problematic.

The reason behind this is that many of them who lived through the civil war enjoyed the abundant gifts of food and medicine America donated to the hungry and the sick. They saw doctors, nurses, and Red Cross workers working for free to save lives. They hadn't seen anything like that before.

From that experience, they made up their minds that America is "a land flowing with milk and honey." I also benefited from the generosity of spirit in the American people during the war. That, I think, helped me to build my own interest in America, of which I am now a citizen.

While I was overenthusiastic about going to America, it took me sixteen years to realize the dream. That was the case because my parents did not have money to support my dream. The idea of going to America in the early 1970s was driven by the prevailing muscles of my pear groups, who had ready financial support from their parents.

On my friends' arrival to the U.S., they mailed countless letters to me and enclosed lovely color photos with their white friends and classmates. Also, they included the unthinkable pictures of them, sitting on the hood of their long and fuel-consuming American cars, perhaps Chevrolets and Fords which all the more captured my interest in an unbelievable way.

At the time, I might have had eccentric concepts about America, but not to the extent of thinking it was a bed of roses. I couldn't make out, however, how a student could own a car when at the time our African teachers had only bicycles and could barely maintain them.

To change their tires and grease the chains for smooth and noiseless ride was a mountainous task for times were as tough as nails.

Readily in my mind was my cousin, Linus who fought side by side with me, writing and asking two of our uncles, who had gone to America, to show us the way.

It did not happen then. Our thinking was different. We never thought of USA to be a continent where we would study, and come back with our heads and shoulders above our counterparts and the community where we grew up.

The very realistic idea we had of America was the story about Dr. Nnamdi Azikiwe, who, we were told, was one of the first Africans who came to the United States of America for studies, and that he supported himself by cleaning people's shoes along the street of New York. We didn't read it anywhere, so if it was true or not, we couldn't tell. But it stuck in our minds forever.

Except Dr. Azikiwe, who, after the Nigerian Independence in 1960, became the first Prime Minister of Nigeria, every person we knew who lived in the United States of America never came home to visit. All of them had their school fees and maintenance sent to them by their parents.

When we began receiving mail from our friends, we learned for the first time that blacks were discriminated against and that they were not allowed to live in certain areas or get a job. The news for us was Greek to our ears. But it didn't prevent us from seeking to be in America.

It was easy, we were told, to get visas for other countries of the world; but the U.S. visa was gold. There were lots of mixed emotions of joy and sorrow for families sending their sons to America. At that time, they never returned; it all ended up in letters and photographs.

It's probable they didn't visit home because they couldn't afford it.

Inspiration may slip—it's our duty to keep it alive and burning. I have had natural interest to travel around the world, and in doing so, my first visit was Rome. In my tour of the city, in a double-decker tourist bus that I never saw before. I was fascinated with the sight and our passage through the River Tiber and the Coliseum, which, visually reminded me of my lessons in Shakespeare's tragic play of "Julius Caesar" and the comparison Cassius draws of Caesar's ambition and tyranny: "Why, men, he doth bestride the narrow world Like a Colossus, and we petty men Walk under his huge legs...."

I wouldn't have had an iota of imagination about the proportional height and size of the statue—Colossus, which William Shakespeare draws his similarity with Julius Caesar, and which underscores some of the vast advantages in traveling.

Chapter 7

My Dreams and My Encounters

It is true that new discoveries are young ambition's dreams. Among the list of my dreams was to be a manufacturer of any type of consumer goods, even if it was a toothpick. Second was to write a book—an autobiography.

Strong in my hunt to be an industrialist, I went ahead to register a business name—Eudomel Industries. At the time of the registration, I had not concluded with what it was that I wanted to produce. Eudomel sounds English. The origin is significant to explain.

It is merely a combination of the first three letters in my wife's middle name, Udo. I anglicized the prefix by importing the letter, "E." The second part of the name, the suffix, is simply my three-letter-name—Mel. That's how the name- EudoMel, was born.

With the business name, I later made good on a few cottage industries, producing: manual candle machines, candles, and tripod gas cookers with circular burners, which earned me both private and state recognition followed by numerous business contacts in the northern states of Nigeria, where I exhibited my wares annually in the national trade fairs that took place in Kaduna, Yola, and Kano. I showed up in the Lagos trade fair only one time. The venture in

Lagos was economically counterproductive, so I stopped exhibiting in Lagos after an ugly experience in the 1988 exhibition.

On the second day of the show, I ended up in a health clinic very sick with food poisoning. At lunch, a restaurant in the trade fair complex served me leftover food from the previous day that made me throw up about three times per minute. It followed with diarrhea, dysentery, and I also suffered from excessive dehydration; that was a killer.

I could not stand on my feet all I did was crawl in and out of the bathroom. I couldn't tell the number of times I was in the bathroom or the length of time that I spent each time.

I almost died if it had not been the concoction of one half cup of warm water with a teaspoon of salt, and half cup of Guinness Beer given to me by my cousin, Josephine, in whose brother's house I stayed each time I visited Lagos for business or vacation. Josephine is sister to my cousin, Dr. Linus Asiegbu.

The potion worked! I stopped vomiting and my diarrhea and dysentery stopped, but I was inestimably weak till the next morning before I was sent to the clinic for hydration. I was given several intravenous dextrose therapies and antibiotics, and spent about eight hours in the clinic. When I got back, I apologized to my cousins for the inconveniences that I caused them.

I had to make calls to my cousins at Owerri, Chief Livinus and Philo Oparah, explaining to them what I was going through because at that time, I contemplated, they would testify to the cause of my death. Otherwise there would be all sorts of silly accusations floating out there.

My experience of the restaurant in Lagos is one of the unforgettable incidents in my life. I came very close to death and is definitely one of the fundamental reasons I am scared of eating in restaurants till today, scared of who cooked the food, how it was cooked and the time it was cooked. Naturally, I have a sensitive stomach and for that reason I prefer to cook my own food.

Through personal enquiries in my subsequent trade exhibitions in other regions, I discovered that the majority of the food sellers were friends, family, or concubines to the organizers, security agents, and what have you.

Some of them paid bribes to the gate and security agents to sneak in. That's how awful it is and you think it's getting better anytime soon? It's still happening to day.

Would you wonder why death rates in the third-world countries are measured in geometric progression and rising? And do you wonder why the average life expectancy in these nations has crashed to all time low?

Governments have some parts to play as do the individuals who eat the foods and drink the water, just like I did out of sheer ignorance.

From personal experience, I grew out of it, but others have not; the health departments are toothless dogs to the people's needs.

In revealing these facts in a more detailed approach, I believe I have done my service to the general public.

I would therefore blame those who have had the same basic and repulsive experience in poor hygiene but have not passed on their lessons.

There are places you could get more facts about the food vendors and they are: All Federal, State, and Local Government Secretariats, except perhaps, in the Federal Capital, Abuja and the Embassies. Literally, all the other grounds, like the market and recreational squires are violently infested with food poison.

There are one or two – perhaps a few more – public water systems in the entire nation. Nigeria is endowed with liquid gold, natural gas and other resources but can not improve the health of its people nor their standard of living.

The illegal food sellers go out every morning carrying food on their heads, sometimes out of cabs, minibuses, and with just about a gallon of water (the source of water is anyone's guess).

Many others bring their food in wheelbarrows. Then, they will disperse to various locations around offices; in open fields, and under the shade of trees where they market their contaminated foods.

They serve the foods with a couple of enamel or plastic plates and after each customer; they would rinse the plates in a common basin of water, which within a couple of hours changes to dark and greasy looks like crude oil.

Only your imagination can come close to understanding the acidic and toxic nature of this liquid, where all the plates, forks, and spoons are washed all day long, at least for eight hours. The result is that every Friday has turned out to be mass-burial holidays of and for civil servants.

Right on top of the colored waters, you could see a host of unlucky flies that forfeit their lives in their try to get a bite or two at the food.

Unquestionably, the stench of the colored water attracts the pests and I wonder why people don't cringe at the sight and smell of the liquid.

Think about it; if the flies eat free and some die in the process, why would the people eat and pay for the same deadly food?

I learned one good lesson from the incident. I make sure that I have at least a bottle of Guinness Beer left in our pantry regularly should I or anyone in my household suffer from food poisoning. Again, the blend of warm water, salt and the Guinness as first aid works like magic.

Our African home is not a conceptual thing; it exists. It's a place, not a space; a place where men, women, and talented children are stock with the inadequacies of a developing continent; where, for instance, there are epidemics of typhoid infection diagnosed in every patient, sick or healthy.

Two days into my summer vacation from the United States to Nigeria, in 2002, I went to a medical laboratory at Aba for a full blood count and my laboratory result was typhoid-positive. I went to a second lab, five streets over, to repeat the test. My result was typhoid-negative. I showed the second lab technician the first lab's results and asked for an explanation – who was right, who was wrong, and why?

The second technician, Godwin, said to me that substandard reagents show every damn blood test typhoid-positive, even when tested with windshield cleaner, or spring water, orange juice, pineapple; etc.

I dived into my second concern of arthritis, which people in the villages say, is perverting not only the old, but also the middle-aged women at home. He satisfactorily tied the major cause of arthritis to the harmful effect of counterfeited medication that is commonly dispensed to the people, added to the high cost of living that's beyond people's affordability.

Mr. Godwin, whom I knew had his education in Houston, Texas, further said women take more medication than men, and so suffer the side effect of the counterfeited prescription drugs for arthritis more than men.

Another issue he added is the numerous childbirths with less-than-adequate prenatal and postnatal nourishments.

We need resolute professionals who are as good as Godwin to be taking care of our parents all year round. Bless his soul, Godwin died in motor accident 2008.

I recall the Legion of Mary, the religious kernel our parents sowed around us as a farmer sows his seeds, teaching us good values, as well as the fear of God, respect to humankind, and public properties. We had little excuse not to bloom as roses of decency and generosity by engaging in some formats that could help save Africa from the replicating persecution of awful governance. Here is our chance not to fail our generation as government has failed the people.

Would a health center without genuine medication help? What reagents would the lab technicians use, and if they want to do blood tests, would there be electricity at all?

Every health-care plan this time must give way to preventive care until the government calls for accountability. If not, the doctors, the nurses, and the storekeepers would be tempted to sell the medication and pocket their loot without question.

The first step we should take toward the good health of the people is to educate them about mosquito nets for their doors, windows, and beds. Also, we should teach them to boil and filter their water and to buy their meat fresh each day before the flies celebrate on them.

Also, it's high time we demanded in writing that government leaders provide functional toilet facilities in all of the market squares.

With our experience and knowledge about the importance of good sanitation, let us insist also on providing restrooms in churches and make it one of the outstanding responsibilities of our age. It's unbelievable; pastors at home don't see the importance of restrooms in the church.

Our people are worthy of healthy environments, and if they are shy to demand their rights from government, we should step in to steer the crusade until their rights have been built as a flagpole on which other social evolutions could be affixed. It is, I suppose, not God's wish that communities in Africa would continue to live in sickness and in poverty eternally.

Little upgrades here and there could go some ways in helping Africa to choose preventive therapy over fake medications that consequently lead to their deteriorating condition of health. If we undertake the project of preventive care, we would have formed brighter, healthier, and happier years of whatever remains of the people's lives and then leave the younger generation with a foundation to build stronger preventive measures in the communities.

I come from a small hamlet, Amuzi, who before the civil war had an individual, a government health agent, my father—Stephen Igbokwe—*nom de plume*, "Nw'oleala" a Public Health Inspector.

In his aptitude as a civil servant, he circulated oral information about good healthy practices and waged war against plant-breeding mosquitoes and dangerous trees. It was his duty to make owners of very tall trees at risk with windstorm cut them down to prevent the trees from damaging their homes or injuring people.

Furthermore, he was on call, around the clock, dispensing unadulterated medication to the sick. He vaccinated children against smallpox, missiles, and hepatitis and treated people's open wounds and rashes that physically abused the young and old. Our night sleeps were in jeopardy if we had the rashes. They were so scratchy that we needed assistance from someone to scratch our backs; otherwise, we would need the tree trunks to do the job.

Days were not our friends; we were at the mercy of flies feeding off the stench of our wet and rash-roasted skin. The rashes were painfully infected and re-infected often without the help of antibiotics, and I wonder today how many of us were able to make it to our adulthood through those awful conditions.

Unmistakably, my father, served his people well and my legacy couldn't have been possible without his influence, in choosing my school for its discipline, in protecting me from dying in the civil war that he believed from his God-given-guts we wouldn't win, and finally, he challenged my desire to stay home instead of fleeing for my life as the war swept across our villages in January of 1970

I would have been killed by the Nigerian army, who shot on sight every young male of my age who they somehow suspected was in combat even when one was not in military uniform. We should not forget that judgments of the jungle are unjust to a growing generation. In addition war is such an evil we should not support.

There were other altruists, who either lost their lives or were maimed for the good of our community. This allusion is in reference to early 1970, when a man was slain in cold blood and another mutilated in their selfless effort to deal with armed robbers that disturbed the peace of our town.

I think we're old enough to pay tribute to those who are worthy of it. If not, what other compassionate matter would persuade our tears to kiss our soil than the memories of those who gave their lives for the rest of us to live healthier and peacefully.

Chapter 8

War Years and Cha-cha-cha

The buildup of my character and behaviors earned me a draft, not into the military for war, but into the seminary, to "learn good behaviors and be successful," my father said.

I liked it and blended into the seminary life without complaining. While in the seminary, I did one thing good that I always remember and treasure till this day. I surrounded myself with far more well-behaved and intelligent boys than me; among them: Jude N. Onynwe (JB); Raymond (Romeo) Okoroigbo; now a reverend; and Everestus Osuagwu, alias Merchant, also a reverend. I played like them; clothed, and joked like them; laughed like Romeo; and had wonderful and unforgettable years with these brilliant individuals.

They made me better than I could have ever been alone. My interest in English literature was ignited by Everestus, whom I asked one evening to help me understand the Shakespearian language. He scored 98% in our impromptu test, while my score was 38%; passing mark was 50%, so I failed the test. Mr. K.B.C. Onwubiko, the author of History of West Africa was our lecturer.

Our literature text book was Shakespeare's Merchant of Venice which starts with: "In sooth, I know not why I am so sad: It wearies me; you say it wearies you; But how I caught it, found it, or came by it, what stuff 'tis made of, whereof it is born, I am to learn..."

I could not make anything out of this crazy stuff at all.

Almost on my knees, I asked Everestus to explain to me the meaning of the first paragraph:

"In sooth, I know not why ..."

"It's simple, Mel, what don't you understand?" Merchant yelled.

"The whole thing," I said.

"It's not written in perfect English grammar, so try to make meaning out of a word or two." Then he explained it to my understanding, and after that, the rest was history.

In our next test, I had 80% and Everestus cheered with me. That is how I picked up my liking for English to this day.

If I failed to communicate and connect with my friend, "Merchant," I would have probably hated English and its subsidiary literature.

This past Christmas vacation, 2008, I spoke to Rev. "Merchant" on phone in his parish at Ogbor Nguru and reminded him the assistance he gave me in our study of "Merchant of Venice" and as I rattled through it: "In sooth, I know not why..." "Merchant" was amazed about my blazing memorization. While I had started the work on this book, I promised him a copy—a creation through the help he gave me in my English literature many years ago.

As much as I tried to be free from fighting my school mates would not stop pinching and taunting me; provoking my confrontational temperament. In the seminary, fighting was absolutely taboo.

My friend, Jude, pulled me out of a compulsory fight when we were returning to school after the end of our first spring vacation, we—seven of us—little, tiny young boys, quizzed ourselves and our suitcases into a cab, a Peugeot station wagon which would take us all the way to our school. The cab driver asked all of us to pay at the beginning of our journey and we all did.

When we arrived at Owerri—halfway to our school, the cab driver singled me out and asked me for my fare. I thought it was a joke. He insisting that I hadn't paid him.

Then I saw the tempest coming and forcefully too. My voice was tiny; I could not be loud as I needed to be

My colleagues said everything that needed to be said and they further swore on my behalf that I paid at the same time with them, but to no benefit. I was shocked! And my classmates were as well.

The cab driver was about my father's age and it shocked me how a father would defraud a small boy in broad daylight.

Acting like a wolf the cab driver pulled out my suitcase and threatened to leave me behind. At that point I felt the weight of the world was down on my shoulders and I was ready to start a fight, not minding he was about three times my age and size. If I shattered his windshield, or hit him with anything, I contemplated; my only defense was the strength of my feet to fly away. Then, I thought about what could happen to my luggage. It was a sticky situation.

Jude reached for his pocket and quickly paid the cab driver.

First I felt Jude added insult to my injury and second that my Angels had left me for the devil to take control of the situation.

My head almost exploded; I never experienced as much headaches before that day.

I was not subject to intermittent anger and grief, but the situation turned me into rage against Jude for supporting a dishonest man to have his way.

I decided not to pay him back and told him just that.

"I don't expect a refund," he said.

And I replied, "Maybe he is your brother"

But he kept quiet about my charge and I was shocked by that.

From then on and all the way to our final destination I became silent and at war with myself about how to handle Jude. My thoughts were: Should I pay him back or not? Would he decide to come at me if I didn't or would he report me to the authorities?

I had unbelievable seizures about a way forward.

At that time, 1964, the value of money (£0.30 British Pounds) was way high up not anyone, except my father, would spend that amount of money for me. I was restlessly concerned and torn between paying and not paying him back and that kept me awake all night long. But I was finally able to regain my composure to a manageable degree. I later reconsidered to pay him back.

But I still doubted me, I, a fervent fighter, had not at anytime in my elementary school years come so far down, so simply in defeat without throwing a punch or a pebble.

It could well mean, I thought, that my father's dream of my transformation was coming noticeably through to my being. I had to let go, but held unto Jude.

By daybreak I concluded how special this boy was and not to pay him back would seriously corrode the ideals for which my father sent me to this particular institution.

It was a test I needed not just to pass; but score with a record distinction; invoking all my elements of humility, I stood before Jude and said: "Thank you, Jude for yesterday," and paid him back.

A guy with few words, replied, "Thank you Mel."

I didn't possess such a desirable quality of calmness and humility as Jude. I would have fought on his side if he was the one in my shoes and I, his witness.

The civil war put our lives on hold and we were lucky to come out of it alive, and since then we have been friends.

It's awful to experience tough times. But without a test of the war any detail about hardship falls on deaf ears.

In early 1966, when Nigeria was in political turmoil, I remember clearly how much Reverend Father Stanly Surff asked every one of us to devote his time in prayer so that we would not get into the mess of war. He emphasized that a nation that fought a war can never be the same. He sighted examples of other nations and explained the problems of refugees, scarcity of the basic needs of life: shelter, food, water, and medicine. But we still wanted war declared; we still wanted to revenge the cold massacre of over 300,000 men women, and children of the eastern region by the northern Muslims.

We, as teenagers wanted to go to war. We didn't think of arms and ammunition to defend ourselves. We had no penknives no bows nor arrows to fight with. We likely would have thrown stones at enemies who carried automatic rifles.

If we depended on throwing stones against our attackers, we would need at least a strong shopping bag to carry so many stones; we had nothing. We would have no savings for the next breakfast, lunch, or dinner. If by chance we had money, a few pennies, stores would not be open; the owners would also be running for their lives and supplies would be looted by hungry refugees.

It didn't cross our minds about what to do if our parents went to war and got killed. People living in the urban cities had no transport fare to return home and those who had cars would be stuck on the highway for lack of gas. All roads would be jammed with people running for their lives, and there would be no food to eat, nor water to drink for hundreds and thousands of miles.

When the war was at full blast, everyone saw the tempests in their full shapes and colors. We could not do a thing to save ourselves, let alone fight. Although there were places in the tropical forest all around us, dense with blankets of tall trees and wide leaves, where we could hide and did from war planes, we couldn't hide from hunger. Nagging hunger kept all of us awake and suffering. Many parents who went out in search of any kind of food or water for their children got buried by cannon fire from the war planes. The worst of the situations, mothers had their newborns die in their palms. Sadness and depression filled our surrounds and if they were commodities; we had excess of the two we desperately needed to throw away. It was too late to pray and nowhere to fly for patronage.

If we managed to get something to eat and filled our stomach, we were still very hungry—hungry to be free from fears, hungry to go back to normal activities, to go back to our schools, and continue a normal life with our friends. It didn't matter how much we dreamt and wished for that normal life to resume, it was far from coming.

The war was three years long. We were stuck in a ditch. Children and pregnant women were the most vulnerable. For lack of nutrition, they died in thousands. Therefore, if you know of a nation at war, pray for it. If you sense that a nation is about to break out in war, don't just pray, do whatever it takes, write; demonstrate, send electronic mail to stop the move for war, especially for the sake of children and pregnant women, dogs, and cats that have no hand in the politics of who is right or who is wrong.

Twelve months into the war, all of us had grown a year older and wiser. School doors were still permanently closed in our region of the country. Teachers and up to 75% of the men had left for combat.

And Amuzi Town continued to be slightly entertaining and eventful with a School of Ballroom Dance, put together by Aloysius 'kwaba. He was also a member of St Jude's school band and when he left school, he stayed in the entertainment industry in Lagos, long before the war.

In the school of ballroom dance, at the northern block of the Holy Rosary Primary School, Mr. 'kwaba taught us the fundamentals of classic dance, the quick steeps, rumba, tango, ballroom, jazz, and what have you. He gave us a gift that we all cherish today.

Because regular schools were out and we had nothing else to do, the dancing practice was the only place we could find a bit of recreation and expression of delight. It came at the time of need, a time when we were hungry and needed identity in the midst of our hunger. Every one of us, who took part in the musicals and dance practices, thought it was one of the best things we could have ever done and continue to be one of those recurring memories of our time.

This definitely accounts for why I give up my dinner for not only watching, but making merry in the TV program: "Dancing with Stars." Given the conventional setup in a remote village like ours, I might not have had the opportunity to know the bare bones of dancing.

We didn't last long in the schedule; the war was getting closer and more frightening also. News about our comrades, who had been killed in different fronts of the war, started filtering into our ears. The news of the dead was considered top secrete, parents of the dead were never informed about their son's death.

At a point we thought that our continuing gathering for the dance schedule could be an ideal target for mobilization into the military and also for air raids, so we parted. In the end we lost many of our playmates in the war.

The most disheartening thing about the war was that the remains of the boys were not brought home for honor burial. My imagination tells me thousands of them were left to rot and decay and others left to be food for scavengers.

Jude and me became very good friends and when I went home at the end of the semester, I asked my father's permission to visit with him in his home. From then we continued exchanging visit every vacation until the Nigerian Biafra war turned our world and everything around us upside down and inside out. At this time I remembered father Surff, who asked us to pray and do whatever we could to avoid the war. Unfortunately we didn't have the power to tilt the state of affairs either way.

Jude signed up for the war, but I didn't. As pugnacious as I was, it surprised everyone who knew me, and who perhaps had a couple of fights with me in the primary school that I did not join in fighting the war.

Although my father had counseled me earlier to be of service to my people when they needed me, I guess he took his opinion back when he was convinced it was bad judgment to engage in any form war.

Not minding what the odds were, I was still zealous to enlist in the army. But as things developed, some degrees of reality were out in the open. The many burials I witnessed made me think twice; one of the dead could have been me. Then my Dad's plea for me to avoid the war at all costs started making sense to me.

I therefore stayed home; even when I was conscripted the first and second time, my interest had diminished so much that it would take a dynamite to uproot my resolve not to enroll and a crane to drop me off in the battlefield. I was convinced I had the right to protect myself from death and I am happy that I didn't give up the right.

I discontinued my military training, first, with the help of a reverend father, now Monsignor, Donald Okoro.

He was our spiritual director in the seminary, before the war began.

During the war, he became the military chaplain with the 63 Infantry Battalion, from where I was conscripted and marched down for a makeshift training.

At the third and last day of our quasi military training in a nearby bush, Father. Donald drove in his Volkswagen Beetle to hear confessions of new recruits who were Catholic, ready to be shipped to the battlefield at midnight.

Three-day training was bloodcurdling. I could have been one of them. In the training camp we neither had good drinking water nor sufficient food to eat. At night, we lay on the bare floor. Our shirts were taken away from us perhaps, to prevent us from escaping. So we neither had our shirts to sleep on the floor nor blankets, nor anything cloth to ward off mosquitoes and the cold breezes of the nights.

We had been told in the most impolite, and loud military tone that we must not complain about anything, they said, "Someone is thinking for you."

If anyone in his right mind did actually think for us and thought about us in the right way without question, he should have been more concerned about our good health first, before tossing us to the warfront.

I mean three-day training, not three weeks; but 3-days of oral babbling, no practical workshop! It was comparable to an unwilling horse taken to the stream for a drink of bad water. That was a joke and I was not prepared to waste my life in the disorder.

Subsequently, we lined up for the confession and at my turn, I knelt down on the confessional box and said at once:

"Father, it's me, Mel, seminarian, conscripted three days ago."

"What happened to your ID?" he asked.

"Father, I showed it to them, but they didn't consider it, but took it from me," I affirmed.

"That's nonsense!" he said, pointing to an adjacent location, east of the primary school hall, about 14 feet from the confessional.

"Wait for me there, till I'm done," he said.

And I waited, standing in a teeth-shattering severe anxiety, blinking my eyes about a hundred times per second.

At least he, Father Donald recognized me, and I was sure he wasn't going to disappoint me for any reason between heaven and earth.

I had absolute hope I was leaving; delightful, that I wasn't going to be the next sacrificial lamb going to war ill-equipped.

To be in the warfront is to fight not as an observer, but fight a more equipped and seasoned enemy without physically touching an arm or ammunition and without any knowledge of how to load and unload a weapon. The "no questions asked policy because someone was thinking for you" made me think the jungle wasn't meant for me nor was I meant for the jungle.

After he was done with the confessions he walked me to the commander of the battalion and signed off on my discharge. I felt his military and religious authorities were profound, influential and indisputable.

The episode earned me a nickname from him. Till to day he calls me "The three-day soldier guy."

Second, with the help of my paternal sister-in-law, Mrs. Maria Emeziem, I was again excused from the improvised military training of the Cobra Battalion.

My father was quick to act; so I didn't spend more than six hours in the camp. This happened in 1968. After 41 years the memory of my conscription and the people who helped me get out of it alive, the experience is still very fresh in my mind.

On Christmas Day 2005, I called Madam Emeziem for Christmas wishes and reminded her how she saved my life and told her how much I appreciated her. She was overjoyed and said she doesn't remember the incident at all. She now lives in California with her husband, Alexander Emeziem, whom I also talk with occasionally.

As the war continued, I later joined the World Council of Churches who flew in food and medicine to the war-distressed people of Biafra.

In the relief distribution center run by the Irish missionaries, we seminarians unloaded trucks of all types of food and distributed them to rural communities and churches.

Each time I remember the relief work we did at the Assumpta Cathedral, Owerri, the name Gerald Anyanwu, my senior in the seminary, now a reverend, sets me off laughing.

He also gave me a nickname: "Fast Guy." He was, and I'm sure he still is, an extraordinarily cool-headed guy I ever met. He stood by watching me; smiled, laughed at me, and shook his head at the quickness I was taking out food items without protocols.

He saw me day after day devotedly ripping up bags of foods and taking the much I wanted without looking behind. Then, one day he approached me to know what I was doing with all the food and I told him frankly that I gave the food out to the Ogoni, Port Harcourt refugees.

Not many of my colleagues could do it without fear. How much could I eat if I did it for me? It was a lot of food. It was a selfless service and I think Father Gerald understood my sympathy for the hungry and left me alone. As my senior, he had the power to stop me, but never bothered me.

I could not stop myself from grabbing as much food as possible for the hungry because while we were climbing on top of food, people on the streets, especially refugees from the delta were starving and I was there to help them as much as I could.

They were brothers and sisters to me, who had nothing to eat and had nowhere to lay their heads.

The few of them that I interviewed told me that they lived on whatever they could get from the bush, hunting for rats and rabbits. When they had killed all rats and rabbits in the bushes, they resorted to hunting down grasshoppers for their daily protein. And when the population of the grasshoppers and caterpillars (young insects) were all out, many more refugees, mostly children died in their teens and thousands.

It could have been me, my parents, or my direct siblings out in the wilderness, looking up in the heavens for daily bread.

The work we did and the experience we came across in the distribution of the food donated by international organizations prepared my mind for more selfless services and goodwill to the needy; even without material donation, I put my voice out there in their favor, optimistic that someone someday will listen to voice of reason and do whatever is necessary to make people happier, healthier and have a contempt for wars.

And it gets me to examining the causes, costs, fears and scars of war as well as any lessons that come from war.

Again, my Dad; without my dad I would be the first set in my age group to hit the warfront. He cautioned me and sent for an uncle, who had fought for two years already to advise me against my attempts to join the army. He feared I would be killed and second, that we weren't going to win the war, the most sincere and honest advice that a parent could give to his beloved son or daughter.

Once again, I listened to him, but not without grumbles and childish ceremonies. I am happy it paid off.

When the war was finally over, as my dad predicted, not in our favor, Jude, my friend didn't return to the seminary. He changed to another school. My appeal to change to the same school hit the rocks. My father said I should go on with the seminary as long as it took.

What I couldn't understand was why Jude, who thought it was wrong for me to fight the cabdriver and prevented me from it, ended up carrying arms and fought the war. I missed my friend, Jude. But we continued our friendship to this day.

Chapter 9

Words Matter

My Restroom
Next to my bedroom my bathroom
A mirror hangs and searches
With mouth so wide, but says not
Too quiet and gentle to nag
But when it shrills, it screeches
It squeaks, squeals, and screams
Clean me or I scream.

At times it takes some well thought out plan to highlight the things children hesitate to do, their environment. Thus the purpose of the above poem to make them realize they need to clean up their mess. In their rooms I would place a different script: My garden has wonderful cabbage; I never saw garbage like this in anyone's room! Communication is most effective when it's composed in substance and style.

I completed my Novel network courses at Moraine Valley Community College, Illinois. I was pathetically new to the computer world—so new that each class assignment in the junior college took me countless hours to complete, while my classmates did theirs right away in class within fifteen to twenty minutes.

From Monday through Friday I took all my assignments home and stayed awake all night to get them done. I hadn't experienced anything like it in my entire life.

I was good, but not perfect in every other thing I had tried. I am not a stranger in sporting activities. I played soccer in my primary school years until I had fracture on my left wrist. That didn't stop me; I shined in track in place of soccer. I also competed in the high jumps, but did not go too far with it.

In high school I ran track: the 100, 220, 440, 880 miters and some mile races. Our trainer called me "A shot from a gun." I represented my school in track meets and came home victorious.

I thought computer education at the junior college level, especially typing, would bend to my "I-can-do-it spirit," which has been carrying me through in my life.

I had a desire for speed in typing, which never happened. I was eager to learn but as much as I tried, I couldn't measure up with my classmates. I did everything to improve, and everything I tried failed. My fingers failed to move as fast as my legs. So if my feet had anything to do with the keyboard I would have done better.

I got frustrated, but instead of quitting school, I quit cab driving. Although cab driving in Chicago was a quick and independent money-making machine, I knew from the onset I wasn't going to lean on it for a long time. I needed to focus on school to take me out of it. But the task at school was excruciatingly challenging and not doing well as I desired made me sad.

Looking at the keyboard left to right, up and down, and not knowing where the letters were was all so confusing. I couldn't differentiate between the number '0' from the letter, 'O.' I looked, pecked and made mistakes while my classmates made music on their keyboards. I was not only embarrassed but nauseatingly miserable. It downed on me that I had a long and daunting way to go. I was in a fix.

I realized I needed both divine help and an earth-bound help, this time from one of my instructors; his name, Mr. Al Munoz. He answered my plea in such a quick manner as if he was waiting for me to ask.

One afternoon, when school was over, I went into his office and told him I needed to be successful in school. The meeting lasted for exactly 30 minutes.

First, he asked me what I needed help with.

In everything; Mr. Al, I replied.

Then he said, "I can't help you if you can't point to one area you need help with."

"Again, I replied, "I don't know what I'm doing in class and the lectures, are kind of above my comprehension."

"What have you done with computers lately?" he asked.

"Nothing, except the time I bought a computer, set it up for my kids, and that's it."

"Don't you type stuff, like letters and don't you play computer games?"

"No!" I replied, never did I lie about my ignorance in computer usage. I told Mr. Al that after taking my time in reading the step-by-step installation process and got my kids set with the computer, I stepped away, afraid that I could ruin the function of the piece of equipment—a tabletop Compaq Presario. "It cost me $1,350.84 in 1986," I emphasized.

"More than anyone in my class, Al, I am serious to learn," I told him.

At that point, he advised I should drop the network studies he was teaching and go down two steps: First, a basic computer course and second, a course in computer hardware before getting into the Novell or Cisco network courses.

According to him, I was like someone who never went to primary school and got into the university to do a master degree program. I didn't know that.

I never knew what I was into except the information I got about the extraordinary salaries of computer network employees which caught my attention. I discovered two ways of meeting difficulties: You revise the difficulties or you modify yourself to meet them. I was into it to get a piece of the pie, not knowing how complex the terrain was.

The junior college might have assumed my high school diploma from a foreign country included computer education which perhaps was basis for my admission.

In Nigeria, we did not have computers in our high schools then. We had typewriters, not for students, but school secretaries. We wrote everything on paper, in pencil and pen, and by hand. We called every pen a Bic, even if it had been made by another company. If we had anything to type at all it would be age declaration only and we looked for a commercial institution to get it done for us at a fee.

So, after completing those preliminary courses as Mr. Al prescribed, I went back in for the software classes I had registered for initially. Al put me on the front burner, making sure I never lagged behind.

From then on, the lectures were coming through; I could then ask questions, and also was able to answer questions using virtual computer terminologies.

I was excited, still sluggish in my typing, but not too far behind in my assignments as was the case the very first time I began.

Behind my confidence was respect from my new classmates, who didn't know me and didn't know my plight, but who sometimes depended on me as I did on them to catch up with the last sentence the teacher altered or the assignment for the next day.

Mr. Al stayed on my case by inviting me to his house every Sunday for hands-on exercises. He was so good to me that when I was done with school and was called to interview for my first computer job in Texas, I remembered I couldn't have passed the interview without his help.

My approach and appeal for his help paid off big-time. I use this illustration to persuade my children to be friends with bright students. Brilliant students emit positive influence on their peers. Secondly, I tell them it's good to make themselves known to their teachers, to tell teachers where they have problems in their subjects and ask for their help. Teachers are invaluable tools; students should not pause to make the most out of them. Words matter a lot.

In school, nothing can be better than using the right tools for the right approach to studies. Words matter to our success.

By and large, from my experience, professors are more than delighted in helping students who are struggling with their studies so that they might be successful, especially when students offer their problems to them. Another tip is that classmates' advice tends to stick more than a professor's 40-minute lecture.

To make your instructors know you by your first name can be key to one's success. Not to do so is a missed opportunity."

Chapter 10

Great Cabbie Episode

I enjoyed driving a cab; of course not at the time I was a novice, when I did not know my way around.

Soon after I started driving a cab, I had a passenger who wanted to go to O'Hare airport.

I was new to the big city of Chicago, after living in Gary Indiana for about 15 months. I visited the windy city of Chicago a few times and loved to live in it.

Before then I had a part-time job, working with a gas station in Merryville, Indiana. My shift was 10 P.M. to 6 A.M.

One night the man, his name was John, who hands over the shift duty to me gave me shocking visit at about 1:00 a.m. He didn't own a car. He had a ride from his friend and the car was packed out of my view.

When the two of them came in John introduced his friend to me and said he forgot to take the empty boxes he wanted for his use.

I said okay, the store is yours, you take them. Still inside the cage, I stood there and watched as they made a couple of trips from the storage down to their car.

In their last trip, I sensed the last two boxes they had were heavy in their arms. So I asked John to stop and open the boxes but he refused.

Almost at a point of getting out of the cage, my instinct pulled me back. I had an internal message what I was witnessing was rubbery and if I opened the cage, they were likely to force themselves inside the cage for cash and perhaps shoot me to death. I didn't take things for granted.

Immediately, I called the police on them; put a smile on my face as I gave police details of the incident.

Then John delayed his going out in attempt to know who was on the phone with me. I told him I was talking to my wife, still pretending I wasn't perturbed by what I saw.

By this time, the police was close by and his friend who stood outside maybe sensed a danger and asked him to hurry out.

The moment they drove off, the police was at their back and cut them red-handed and handcuffed them. Then as they were arrested two other police officers brought back the boxes John dad stuffed with all kinds of merchandize during his afternoon shift.

When the police told me I was lucky and asked me how I managed to escape the danger it downed on me the news would have been one of sadness. So from inside the cage, not ready to come out, I was terribly horrified and asked the police what I should do. They saw me shaken and asked me to give them the telephone number of the owner.

They called the owner and to my hearing narrated the robbery incident to him and told him I was afraid to stay.

The owner spoke with me and asked me what I wanted to do and I told him I was leaving. He then demanded to talk to the police again and I understood he asked the police to stay with me until he came to calm me down.

I hadn't caught a thief before in my life and wasn't expecting a thief would be someone I knew, working with me in the same office. I was lost in terror.

At mid-day I came to the owner and told him I was quitting, but he said he wasn't letting me go; that he was going to raise my pay and some other promises he made. Those promises fell on deaf ears.

My fear was that John and his friend would come after me when they were done with their police case. That was how my plan of moving down to Chicago began.

I fled to Chicago and meet a friend who was in cab business to get me into the system.

Soon, I found out it was not easy at all. I passed the cab driver's test on my third attempt. I had limited knowledge about distances and the location of passengers' destinations. To get a comprehensive understanding of the city's streets turned out to a binary equation I had to solve with a lot of memorization.

At the beginning I confessed to my passengers that I was still knew and depended on them to direct me to their destinations. But I got into trouble when my passengers were visitors to Chicago like me. Many of them got mad and got out of my cab with a bang at the passengers' door. Some yelled at me while others said, "Don't worry; you'll get it right soon."

So, when the O'Hare passenger got in my cab, I zoomed off for the only airport I knew – Chicago Midway. It was also the airport I landed after our short stay in Dallas, when we first came to the United States.

About halfway there, the passenger was worried and asked it there were two ways to the airport. I boorishly said yes, thinking he was wrong and I was right.

When we got there, at Midway airport he was extremely mad at me and roared, "Where in the world is this, I need to be in O'Hare, not here!"

A feeling of sympathy hit my nerves; I was motionless and quickly apologized to him while transferring him to another cab. I would be lost with him if I attempted to go to O'Hare from Midway airport. My map reading skill of the city was no where close to the connecting route from Midway airport to O'Hara at all. I was miserable and if there was anything I could have done to change the horrible situation to better, I would.

I stood like a dead wood and watched them drive off. He didn't pay me and I didn't ask to be paid, either. If that made him feel okay, I premeditated, his grudges against me would be momentary. I wished him good feeling as they drove away.

On that note, I had some relief and drove back downtown, all attentive to O'Hare calls with the objective not to take any passenger to O'Hare. I didn't know where it was or how to get there from inside the city.

The map reading was a too complicated for me to understand. Moreover, I hadn't lived in Chicago to go from known to an unknown. The downtown Chicago one-way streets offered me another headache and its array of police officers with their traffic tickets at every corner were intimidating. They also lay wait for us up to Grand Avenue and East Jackson Boulevard.

Lakeshore Drive was also home for the police when there was less traffic, north or south bound. Those guys were feverish and never blinked when we fell into their traps.

I noticed afterwards that the police were stricter on cab drivers than other drivers. To prove my point, there were two separate instances when police officers stopped me for moving violations along Lakeshore drive, heading home to my North Side apartment; then on North State Street as I drove my kids to the skating rink. In each case, instead of traffic tickets I got oral warning. I was like, really! Is this a dream with Chicago police?

I was the same person, the same modest accent, the same hair style; not in suite or tie. I would be written up and affronted if I was driving a cab.

Despite the police harassment, I fall back to some of the positive outcome in my few years of driving a cab.

I still have a letter of appreciation that a Californian resident wrote to me about summer of 1995. The wife, in the company of two other women forgot her purse after they dropped off at the Planetarium.

She had reasonable amount of cash in the purse, credit cards and a checkbook, from where I copied her home phone number. The husband's mail reads:

"Dear Mel,
Given the way things have turned out, I could not believe that there are still people like you living among us. I thought it was all in a dream after receiving your

phone call all the way from Chicago informing me my wife left her purse in your cab.

I called my wife immediately and directed her as you said to Yellow Cab lost and found office at 2230 South Michigan Avenue, where she claimed her purse and all the contents were intact.

We are enclosing a $100 check in appreciation for your good will. Thank you so much."

In addition, cab driving not only made me connect with people of all states and nationalities, religious and political spectrum, it taught me the zillion streets, offices, hotels, restaurants and how to navigate the Chicago suburbs in the way I could not have if I lived there for a century.

One of the most heinous crimes that took my breath away – before I started driving a cab – was the Brown's Chicken massacre, on Jan. 8, 1993, in Palatine, Illinois., a suburb of Chicago. In this crime seven people were murdered in the restaurant.

When I started driving the cab I drove down to Palatine to see where the crime took place and to come to grips with the reality.

At that time it was an unbelievable feeling for me that such a crime could take place in America, which I thought was as safe as heaven, with the police presence at the turn of every street, homes and businesses.

"If it could happen in Palatine, it could happen anywhere," said one residents of Palatine.

Chapter 11

My Encounters with the Police

First, in late 1980s, ten years before I immigrated to the States of America from Africa, I foolishly fought with three armed policemen at a particular point called "Mango tree checkpoint," in Aba, one of the commercial nerve center, southeast of the Niger in Nigeria. In the incident, the policemen put-up a roadblock, went to a liquor bar, and got themselves drunk. The nails on a piece of wood they put on the road punctured two of the cab driver's tires.

We were in route for the doctor's clinic on behalf of my sick brother, Ted, who had very high fever -103.2°F, seizure, and later diagnosed with acute malaria.

It was already dark, at about 9 p.m., so when the cab driver came around the corner, he drove over the nails. The cab driver first slowed down, stopped, honked his horn and thought it was okay to continue because there was no sign of police.

Within a flash of a second his two tires were out of air and physically disabled.

When I came out of the cab, I saw three policemen walking out of the liquor bar. They must have heard the noise of the accident and as soon as they saw it was a cab (they make a living out of cab drivers) they descended on the driver as lions would on his prey.

Their immediate accusation was that he refused to stop on their order. They lied; and heavens could have joined me in the testimony. They were not present when it happened.

Before this incident, I never thought the police would lie in their federal uniform. Therefore it was another shock to me after the accident as the police told the gathering public that the driver nearly ran them over at the time they said they signaled him to stop and "he refused."

Offended with the cold dark lie of the night, I stepped forward to one of them asking him why they would set such a dangerous object on a public road without warning and without illumination, and then set out to drink. I laid emphases on "drink."

They smelled alcohol and blabbed unintelligibly without a stopping. What they said didn't make sense and they were ready to fight and I was geared up to lead the battle with that level of frustration. While in the mess, I forgot entirely my sick brother at the back of the cab.

Not to brag about it because it hurts that I over-reacted; I used the same wooden obstacle that deflated our tires and regrettably rammed it on the head of the officer who struck me with his baton.

In a snap of a second he was covered in blood and the other officers and witnesses came to our rescue. The situation was charged. It was so ugly that I don't like to remember.

As if it was a magic, I remembered Dele Udo, a University student at the Enugu campus of the university of Niggeria, Nsuka, who was shot and killed by the police. The incident was still fresh in all the national news. That triggered students' unrest across the nation and universities across the country were shut down indefinitely.

Dele's death was reminiscent of Rodney King's case in Los Angels, 1991, concerning police use of excessive force on a civilian.

Dele's death was reminiscent of Rodney King's case in Los Angels in 1991, concerning police use of excessive force on civilian.

On hearing the word, "drunk," I had hit them where it hurt them most. They were enraged with me because it is against their bylaw, which says, "Drinking alcohol on duty is cause for summary dismissal."

In that anger, mixed with the influence of alcohol, they made a mistake to engage me in a furious fight.

One of them hit me with his baton to shut me up, which woke my long locked-up game of primary school fighting and the key to unlock it was not far from reach.

With an unbelievable childish mentality, I was one of the many Nigerians that vowed to avenge the death of Dele Udo anywhere I perceived police brutality. Shockingly, I narrowly missed a chance of being killed and so were the police in that tempting night.

At that time, I thought that such an act by the police against defenseless civilians was only possible in an underdeveloped nation. That is why Rodney King's case took some blood off me. I couldn't believe it.

As often as I remember my encounter with the police in Nigeria, I regret it a million times over. Simply put, the encounter was a case of transferred aggression off Dele's case.

By my thoughts, "fighting it out" isn't an avenue for proper behavior or a way to nation-building.

Not bothered about what could have happened to me, if I killed the policeman, I deeply reflect that he could have been either someone's son, someone's husband, or perhaps, someone's father and I would have been the one soul in the world to put the family in such an unforgettable and unforgivable situation for the number of years the family would live on earth. It hasn't been easy for these thoughts to leave me. There's no word to describe it In English or French; the feelings won't go away even as I think time will take them away.

Thank goodness we both came out of it alive. Today I believe it wasn't the right thing to do, no matter the provocation. In my feelings, if I could ever find out the officer's name I would like to meet with him and apologize to him about what happened.

Could I have survived it if it was in America? That has a yes-and-no answer. The risks are the same in the dark and bright continents of the world.

Even as I am concluding this chapter I cried over the news about the four police officers in Oakland California shot by a gun man on Saturday, 21 march, 2009. My mind went straight, thinking these officers might be someone's son, someone's husband, or perhaps, someone's father, brother, or son-in-law.

The conscience and the strength of a nation depend largely on the police force and the judiciary. Without them, we have no government, no piece, and no life. It doesn't matter the level of provocation; it's never justifiable for one to take laws into his hands as to shoot or kill the police.

I have also had an encounter with the police in Chicago which was as a result of misunderstanding.

Many years after my ordeal with the police on the other side of the Atlantic, if anyone told me that at the heart of Chicago – Michigan Avenue, in front of Marshall Field's–that I would say anything to a police officer other than "yes sir," I would have doubted him a million times.

Here's what happened: The police told me that I shouldn't have parked where I was. It was at the peak of Christmas shopping, the last weekend, three days before Christmas. I had finished shopping with my family and I asked them to wait for me at the entrance as I went to get our car.

So I replied to the officer that I didn't intend to park, but just stopped to have my family come into the car. As I was talking to him, two of my children jumped in the car. Waiting for their chance were my wife and two other older children. With one of the passenger's doors still open, the police insisted I should leave even as my wife and my two daughters were about two feet away from the car.

"Do you understand English?" The police asked me with frenzy.
"Yes sir, I do." I answered.
"Would you be patient with me, sir, it will only take a minute?"
"No!" He answered.

Again, I asked him to allow the rest of my family to get into the car.

Once more, he yelled at me saying: "Do you understand English?" "May I see your driver's license?"

I replied, "Yes sir" and pulled out my driver's license—holding it out for him to "see." At that point, my entire family was inside my cab.

Then he angrily, bent over and looked at my face through the window, and repeated, "Can I see your license?"

"That's what I'm showing you, sir." I replied, "Unless you want me to *give* you my driver's license.

Then, he said, "Yes that's what I mean."

There and then, he realized that maybe the guy behind the wheel had a better understanding of English language than he thought.

My dad used to tell me that it's stupid to say no to one with a gun. For some reason, I forgot, but I remembered it soon enough.

What I take out of it and my advice to everyone is not to face up to the police even when you think you are right. They are there for us when we need them. They are our heroes and heroines too.

Chapter 12

Caring for Marriage

I married my wife and my wife married me while she was still in nursing school with Our Lady of Lourdes Hospital in Ihiala, south east of the river Niger and I, a civil servant with the Board of Inland Revenue, Aba further south of the Niger river.

In their school they were not allowed to marry until after their graduation. The rule was stiff and not only the school walls were high and hard to climb, it was fortified by the ridged principles of a catholic administrator—an ordained reverend sister well-groomed to take care of spicy teenage girls. She took nothing to chance in watching over the girls. But in some way I managed to hurdle over the parapet with love light wings.

The nursing school was a three-year program and our courtship ran for the same period of time. There was hardly any week that passed by without my presence on the college grounds. BC's girl friends were all entertaining as much as I was; so we found our matches in one another.

Given the situation I discovered why it is as easy as anything for anyone to mess around with the cluster of beautiful young girls who didn't need further introduction of who you are, where you come from and what you are about. It requires silver-coated discipline to overcome the attraction and still be enormously friendly with all of them then and years after.

In our teenage years while in high school we venerated love letter writing to our girl friends. We bragged about it. But it was not easy to come by a girl who was willing to be friend with you. If we were lucky the best way we started was letter writing. Through letter writing we weighed the slope of our persuasion. Usually boys took the first step in writing to the girls and then calculated the number of days it would take for the mail to reach, a day or two to elapse for her to answer and perhaps another four of six days given on its way back. We didn't like the weekend interference with our mails.

Today instant messaging and text messages have taken the highroads. We didn't even have the luxury of overnight delivery which would have served us better if it existed in our time.

As teenagers we didn't have much to pray for except our studies and for the reply of our girlfriends' mails.

When the letter finally arrives we handled it in the same way birds handle their eggs. Our girlfriend's letters were such a pull of exhibition we didn't want anyone to ridicule us about. We first looked for a hidden place to open the mail and made sure we read it first, for its content and then for any grammatical error you wouldn't want anyone to see.

Unfortunately, in an all-boys' school as ours there was hardly any place we could hide to read our letters except in the toilets. The pit toilets might have been replaced with the modern water system, up to today I still visualize the particular toilets where I red my secret mails and the pits that still hold the shredded mails of the girls who either refused my application for their friendship with me or those whose mails I considered might fail the test of group exhibition and admiration. If I knew then what I know now, I would have saved the mails for my library albums.

It seemed we had outbreaks of epidemics in the phrasing of the letters we wrote to our girl friends: "I love you pass my mother," was top on the list.

"I hope you are swimming in the ocean of good health," and then, "I will not sleep until I get your reply."

Sometimes we would smear some kind of liquid on the body of our mails to represent our true tears of thoughts and emotion for them and if that didn't capture the girls' attention, we considered that energy and the allure as lost.

Luckily, coming out of the numerous letter-writing experiences with my girlfriends while in high school, I called up the skill in the true sense of love and showered BC with words of love other than the high school reproduction. I don't know what she did with mine, I saved all her letters and on the file folder holding the mails it has, "Memories are Made of These."

Zelda Fitzgerald, of Montgomery, Alabama, a novelist once said "Nobody has ever measured, even poets, how much a heart can hold." Some of our acts we thought were stupid were not all that unintelligent; we look back and see them as banks from where we draw same knowledge to deal with our present. The bank comes handy when the honeymoon is over and the weight of economic and social responsibilities sit directly at the center of our living rooms; and when the journey of bringing up the children and seeing them through college seem intimidating in a crossroad of culture that has two signs: "Lost," and the second, "Can't be Found."

One other important treasure I earned during my cab occupation was about preservation of marriage. I agree that classroom education earns us certification, but we earn satisfaction by interacting and sharing our life experience with one another.

About five years before I married, I was fortunate to be friends with married families from whom I gained early insight of what marriage was like. The couples were Coleman and Bridget N., who later were guarantors in my marriage. Then, Aloysius and Scholar E., Aloysius died 2007 after a brief illness.

Marriage was at least six million miles away from my mind. I was still thinking of going back to the seminary, where I had planted my image to march along with my most valid friends, without them, I contemplated my pleasure would be broken.

When I was a young civil servant, I was vibrant, stylishly dressed and traveled all over, especially to middle-class marriages. I was elected master of ceremonies or best man. With this setting, I was openly thrown into the center of marriage discussions. There were countless times in those weeding ceremonies when people asked me discomforting questions on when I was going to invite them for my own wedding. My answers were: "Not anytime soon.

In reality, I could not imagine myself dealing with the troubling issue of barrenness that was and still is common in many marriages today. I also couldn't come to terms with the demoralizing effect of infidelity, which was the second most common cause of divorce; and above all, I was intolerably nervous about the strenuous responsibility of raising children from the very minute that they are born until they are at least 18years of age. I thought I was not intended for such demise.

As much as I tried to run away from marriage issues, Coleman, Bright, Aloy and Scholar steadily overwhelmed me with the challenge to, "get married soon." I needed a school of thought for it. And I had only one friend. But I had been told one chooses from a list of friends.

At this time, I had no real pal for consideration in marriage and genuinely disclosed it to Coleman, my childhood friend, who is also my role model. For him that was not enough excuse not to marry within the timeframe they were expecting me to marry and start a family. He stopped at nothing in supporting me in every way to dispel my reservations of being a husband and a father.

Good friends are not easy to come by and so if I began a list project it could have taken me one to two years, or more, who knows. I ended up not having a list. I had one prudent choice to make, to marry my friend.

Although it takes two to tango, it does take a multitude of people across the world, irrespective of class dissimilarity to build a strong and happy family.

In my 26th year of marriage, this year, I have not stopped to learn and to listen to the voice of experience and reasoning toward polishing the relationship with my wife and the exigent methods of raising my children with strong family values, believing that no one is an island.

Surprisingly, though, sometimes it works out that way, other times, it doesn't.

I was not confident stepping into marriage; today I have turned my early fears of marriage into strength and have become better and better as a husband to my wife and as a father to my children through the inclusion of other people's experience in both good and bad lights. For example, when I learn about the reason behind fallen marriages, I fasten my belt, adjust my manners, and if my wife is in such a difficulty that might ruin our affinity, I help her out in many ways, including throwing in some sense of humor to ignite smooth and suiting sense of continuity.

Caused by unknown factor, undeniably, sometimes marriage relationship can go cold in an otherwise a bright summer day.

In some other circumstances the presence of children can also present pleasant diversion and juicy sources of comedy to peaceful relationship within the household. With its epileptic tendencies you could also go crazy after a few minute of utmost excitement.

I also gained enormous experience from many people that received my taxi services, especially one middle-aged man, Rick. Rick hired me from O'Hare airport for three different destinations: first to downtown Chicago, then to 64 hundred block, north of the city, and to, Oakbrook, Chicago North West suburb. By this time I could drive around Chicago downtown and suburbs with my eyes closed.

In the duration of the trip, Rick engaged me in unexpected levels of conversation and my sharp rejoinders made him relax very well with me in such a way that he told me his family problems. He told me in confidence that he made the greatest mistake of his life in the divorce of his first wife.

When I asked him what went wrong in their marriage, he broke down; his voice changed and rings of tears took control of his eyes as I looked at him from my rear mirror. He shook his head from east to west, lamenting that it was his fault. At that moment, I pulled over to take in his emotion.

I couldn't figure out exactly what to do for him. However, we continued the journey for about a quarter of an hour in dead silence before he altered, "I'm sorry."

"That's okay," I said.

At the end, he counseled me never to argue with my wife for whatever reason, stating that he lost his marriage with his first wife because of tireless arguments with her even when he was convinced his argument was unnecessary.

In my mind, I said, "We all do it." Maybe I was worse in argument with my wife than the God-sent passenger; I didn't need any human sacrifice to engrave his peril into my being.

As soon as I secured the money he paid me, I took off and headed straight to my apartment with an undertaking not to argue with my wife even when there is need for argument. But I still think it's practically impossible for married couples not to argue in favor of one political party against the other or disagree with one NFL team or another and sometimes a television station to watch. When an argument with my wife becomes practically irresistible, I quit deliberating on my passenger's invaluable advice.

One example, though it's nothing that pulls off a strand of hair was a time my wife accused me of not wiping down one half of our bathroom mirror; the section I use, next to my faucets. She alleged I splash water on the mirror.

I told her the watermarks are formed out of the mist from the shower. But she did not believe me and insisted on her position.

So about three months later I came back to the point about the mist on the mirror, suggesting she didn't clean my side of the mirror while I was away for several months.

She said: "That's not true; how you dare think that is possible? I couldn't have done half the mirror and left the other."

"That's my point," I said. "If you cleaned both sides in my absence, who then used my side of the mirror when I wasn't at home; don't you agree with me now that it's the mist off the shower, not me?"

She had no explanation to it and that ended the issue. By all estimation, a four-hour lecture couldn't have been more practical and more significant to me than my passenger's advice not to argue with my wife.

Arguments are difficult to avoid; it's great fun to have a home where husband and wife for example mutually differ in their support for different political parties, different football or basket ball teams in order to give piece a chance.

An Irish saying affirms: "A quarrel is like buttermilk, once it's out of the churn; the more you shake it, the sourer it grows". It also says "You've got to do your own growing, no matter how tall your grandfather was." It's good we make our points and leave matter at no victor, no vanquished conclusion.

Chapter 13

Point of Reference

The beginning of understanding is the breakthrough of something we do not comprehend. Fellow Americans ask me where I'm from originally, and why I came to America, in particular, Chicago—the Windy City. And that was when I lived there for nine years before moving down here in the Villages of Woodland Springs. I have not played dumb to the questions. I have sincerely answered them satisfactorily, each time—reciting the same reason that has evolved to a more detailed story telling.

Each time I told my story, I noticed my questioners are not in a hurry to leave. Ninety-nine percent of them have no passport and therefore have not traveled beyond the boundaries of the United States of America ever in their lives. That surprises me a lot.

One would think that the upbeat and buoyant Americans would have traveled the whole world. Hug!—just kidding.

I have visited: Rome, United Kingdom, Taiwan, and Singapore, including the United States, where I have also visited two dozen states out of the 50.

Of course, traveling to foreign countries for a visit is one thing – but living in a foreign country is quite another. It is adventure filled with situations to which I would react one way in Nigeria, but have learned to react quite differently in the United States. For example, consider my story regarding my brother-in-law, Rev. Matthew Iwuji, three months into my stay in the US.

One Sunday morning as I was riding with him to Crown Point, Indiana where he usually visited with elderly couple, who lived by themselves and could not attend Sunday services.

Suddenly, on that lonely stretch road from Gary, a mighty deer jumped out of the bush west of us, crossing to the opposite side of the road, and I yelled as loud as I could for Father Matthew to hit him head-on. Instead he stepped on his brakes. He astonishingly stopped for the big animal to go about his business and I was shocked beyond expression.

Then I was quiet for about one minute and asked him why he did that. As if it was not a serious subject, he smiled at me and calmly showed no emotion and asked me what I would have done with it if he killed it. And I exclaimed with my arms up to roof of the car: "Eat it for breakfast, lunch, and dinner!" And he replied, saying that I certainly will be tired of eating meat by the time I lived in this country for one year. But I doubted him.

I have always told my stories to many Americans at work and to neighbors including strangers in shopping malls and recreational places, and they enjoy my humor as I give out my intercontinental experience of life as I have seen and lived it from way-back-when.

First, I notice evidence of wrapped attention in their body language. At the end they want to know the difference between America and Africa, which, by the way, is not a country, but a continent with 53 countries in side it, excluding the four islands.

From the experience of the 2008 Presidential campaign, whether it was like a shaggy dog story or ignorance, I would no longer take it for granted; I would be going all-the-way to explaining one of the most significant geopolitical differences between Africa and the continent of North America.

It's common knowledge that the power of American society depends largely upon the interaction between different groups who live in it. Thomas Carlyle, a Scottish satirical writer calls it 'Organic filaments'—elastic threads which helps to bring disintegrating elements together and reunite them.

On a humorous note, contrary to anyone's claim of seeing Russia from Alaska, the continents of Africa and North America are broadly separated by enormous body of water—the Atlantic Ocean and is about 7,300 miles apart.

The details I provide in this book give you an image about the people and culture in many countries of Africa.

"Do you like it here?" They also ask.

My response, "Yep, sometimes!"

"Are you married?"

To tickle their imagination, I say, "Yea, sometimes."

"Why sometimes?"

Then I add, "Just kidding!"

"How many children do you have?"

I say four and then they ask, "By one woman?"

I say of course by just one and not one and a half.

Bill Watterson, an American cartoonist rightly said that a little rudeness and disrespect can elevate a meaningless interaction to a battle of wills and add drama to an otherwise dull day.

And this takes me to a woman postal worker in Gary, Indiana, who showed a lot of interest in my baby each time I stepped into the post office to buy stamps or mail my letters. Mobile phones and electronic mails were still far away in African horizon then, 1990-1992.

That was in 1990, my first year in the United States. I usually carried my baby, Stephanie, in a pram and the postal worker would take a minute or two to talk to her and made her smile. I liked it.

However, one day she baffled me with a silly question, asking if we have airports in Africa.

"What country in Africa?" I asked. But she couldn't name one. It is my guess other continents outside Africa have little knowledge that Africa is made up of 53 countries, not states.

I thought that the postal staff was crudely insulting. So I quickly gave her an answer I am sure she will never, ever forget.

There were at least seven people behind me in line waiting to be attended. Looking back and forth, I replied with a ray of smile: "Mom, we don't have airports in Africa, but whenever we want to fly, we just stretch out our arms like eagles and off we go."

I related the postal worker's ignorance of international experience to a young man from the Middle East who came to America, and a few days later was asked whether the moon in the sky was a full moon or half moon and he answered, "I just came to America a few days ago."

The young lady postal worker did not see the sarcasm coming. All she did was gaze at me and didn't utter a word.

Not being fluent in spoken English, many people think, immigrants don't know much. It is a mistake for anyone however, to assume that someone with an accent is foolish or less of a human. Accent exists within the north and south, east and west of a given nation too.

When I came newly to the United States, I had drama with my mechanic who couldn't understand my terminologies as I couldn't understand his too. A bit of sign language helped us out.

In England and Africa we refer to car trunks as car boots and have spanner for wrench. So when he asked me where my wrench was, my mind went blank. I couldn't understand him. He then explained what he meant by wrench. I never heard of wrench or trunk before. I thought he said truck. Through his explanation I pointed to him what he was looking for was in my boot. He exclaimed, boot!

In Texas, I couldn't understand the meaning of: "I 'm fixing go lunch or fixing to go to lunch." In a given country differences in accent and terminology exist.

Despite the difficulties in accent and terminology, America is to me, the best place in the world and I am proud I am an American.

Not quite long ago, a colleague at work confronted me with the news he heard on the television about 419—a chain of swindlers across Nigerian who have fed fat from defrauding the get-rich-quick foreign nationals by luring them to Nigeria or anywhere in Europe for one kind of multibillion-dollar business deal or another. By the way, the 419 is the section of the law by which the criminals are prosecuted and punished if they are found guilty.

"Mel, would you tell me what you know about the Nigerian 419ners?" he asked.

"Yes," I answered, "they" were in the news last night; I watched it." I inflated, to put out the prejudice and then went on saying: "I do know the overall guy in charge of the 419 in Nigeria was a manager with Enron in Houston for many years before relocating to Nigeria." I exaggerated again, turning the table around. I waited for his answer. But he chilled away.

We have been told often that prejudice is the child of ignorance and if that if we think education is costly, we should try ignorance. Therefore, if anyone wants to know about the world, he should learn about it in a particular sequence. What is pious in the American culture is how the law handles corruption. Here, in America no one is considered above the law. But in Africa the laws are tilted in favor of the powerful and the connected, which is why there has been no light at the end of the tunnel in African countries.

To be explicit, there's no nation that's free from evil. The reason is that humans are the most difficult creatures to control. It doesn't matter how harsh the law might be or how high the walls of the penitentiary are raised, people do whatever they want to do with little regard for the societal norms.

A typical example of how unpredictable people can be is the Jonestown Massacre on Nov. 18, 1978 in the country of Guyana, in South America, where over 900 men, women and children perished under the guise of religion.

Also men have killed their wives for other women and for insurance benefits. Women have killed their children for one reason or another and have claimed insanity.

In Africa, politicians always take laws into their hands. They kill their opponents in other to emerge winners. Crime is everywhere you turn the corner without investigation. Being critical about one crime and having a blind eye on another is as cruel as it is hypocritical and shameful.

The third world, especially Africa would have been a more decent place to live, but widespread corruption has made it absolutely impossible for habitation.

Institutional corruption in government is as destructive as hard drugs. Therefore war against corruption should be fought with the same concentration as the war against drugs. The world is in a race and we want to make sure we are competing on both fronts without our brakes on.

We grew up at a time our parents didn't allow us to attend social events at night. They thought that immorality was the product of darkness and, to a great extent, we believed them.

Nonetheless, at a time I couldn't resist the temptation of getting my hands on the sensation of the midnight extravaganza, I sneaked out of our house through a window and set out for a midnight party.

Electricity was not common at the time; it was spectacular to see the dancing hall festooned with different colors of light bulbs shining on the faces of angels of beauty. The light they had was from a small generator.

Ladies would either be admitted free or have their gate fees paid for them by their boyfriends. As poor high school students, we barely afforded our gate fees and to buy chicken wings for any girl was way beyond our affordability. We would be lucky if any lady allowed us to dance with her, free of cost.

The situation has changed greatly these days because parents are included in almost all the activities of their children within and outside their school. Modern parents also know that it's not only at night that evil is most dangerous.

I was considered a good boy at a particular time in my teenage years. The reason behind the episode was simply not that I could choose right from wrong, the circumstance of the time that particular day vindicated me.

My father sent me on errand when my associates went on with our frequent monkey business; usually the things which would make you shy away when you hear about them.

It was common practice for our elementary school teachers to order us, children to bring whatever was needed in school. We never thought of buying them, instead we went out to hunt for them; not minding it could land us into trouble with the owners.

We stole whatever little item our teachers wanted us to bring for school. This time our teachers had ordered everyone to bring a pineapple sprout to help expand the school's pineapple orchard. In going to please our teachers my friends were caught filching pineapple sucker from one aunty Fidelia's garden. Aunty Fidelia was a woman who had been married from our village a long time ago, but was later bundled back home by the husband because of her mental illness.

When the pineapple sucker issue came up she went round the neighborhoods screaming the names of the boys' and labeled them thieves while at the same time telling everyone she met that I was the only good boy around the bloc.

Because I was not caught among the act with my playmates instantly made me a good boy in aunty Fidelia's assessment, but it at the same time estranged my relationship with my peers. I don't think any radical group of boys or girls for that matter likes to acknowledge a "Holier than thou" in their midst. It threatens their chemistry.

I did everything extraordinarily gutsy to make up for my group expectations to prove that I was still very much one of them in order to revoke the "good boy" status I got from aunty Fidelia. Definitely I had no choice otherwise I would be a lone star.

For that reason I gave more time to acting up in order to be on equal standing with them. As I engaged in various mischiefs the rest of my peers stood by watching and beamed at my success. But the success was momentary.

Although I had the most terrific experience which brought me back into my peers' fold—the "Operation boy come down," I almost made a wrong decision which I would have lived to regret. I nearly jumped from a tree top which could have maimed me for life.

I planned and led the plucking of someone's guava fruits, not knowing the owner lay somewhere watching over it from a distance. Because of the fear of loosing my foothold among my pairs, I did not hesitate to jump onto the tree and in a flash; I was way up to pluck the fruits.

Suddenly, I heard a loud command, "Hay, boy, come down!" Luck ran out on me. It was a do or die consideration, but I choose the former.

The owner of the property came, brandishing his razor-sharp, silver-edged machete above his head, hooting at me to come down at once. I was about 20 feet up on the tree and my peers fled for their lives without looking back. Initially, my heart hammered my rib cage to submission and my nerves trembled. I thought of jumping off the tree, but quickly put the idea off my mind because I wouldn't survive it or if I did by chance, could be maimed in such a way I might not be able to do what I enjoyed doing best—race. I trusted myself and what my feet could do as soon as they had contact with the ground. If I had the chance to land them on the ground, I would fly like a jet. If my attacker knew I could fly like a butterfly he wouldn't give me any opportunity to perch on the ground. He might have heard that my parents have a son no one could outrun at school. But couldn't figure out who was on his property. As growing children, we all looked alike.

I thought of urinating on his head, but that would bring my parents to the sight and perhaps make the matter worse.

As the man continued to yell at me to get down, I climbed further and further up, until he set off climbing to deal with me on the tree branches. Then I knew I had a chance of ideal escape.

I saw that my only option was to escape through a palm tree, whose fronds were easy for me to get a hold on for a quick leap and a slide to the ground. I took that option.

To make sure that the man didn't read my mind, I fiddled a move to an opposite direction from the palm, convinced I wasn't going to cause him to get back down. My thinking was that if he went down to wait for me, I wouldn't have as much chance of escape at all. So I lured him to climb further up.

When he was half way up, knowing that he wouldn't risk jumping off from the height he was, I snapped my organized move onto the palm frond and in a second my weight caused the frond to plunge close to the ground and from there I jumped down like a squirrel. It was magical and I am convinced he hadn't seen anything like it and perhaps watched me with his mouth agape.

I noticed that my feet barely touched the ground as I fled from my attacker. So I had a run of my life and it was the last act that got me enveloped with my peer group. As life went on with us, we went on with life, one day at a time.

Yet, many years later, you look back to evaluate the things you did and realize you have some misgivings about them.

There are many things we took for granted; infringement and violation of privacy were some of them.

When a friend was robbed in his house in 1996, he said to me, "Mel, it's not so much about the television and some other household property stolen from my house that bothers me, that some one or group of people thought about me to the point of braking into my house at night is a dagger to my privacy."

I sympathized with him without realizing the full extent of his frustration, until I had the same experience of theft in my house in Africa. The most frustrating situation about it is being handicapped with the law in a lawless nation such as Nigeria where the police feeds on bribe and does nothing useful with suspects and criminal evidence, rather they destroy them.

Anyone can be a fool, but a fool at 40, we're told, is a fool forever. Here is one of those incidents, when you read about them you wonder if it was real.

I was coming back from Kaduna in 1985, after a wedding of my wife's friend, Evangeline. About three hours in the journey my car had an engine problem that brought it to a stop, north of the River Niger.

In the car were my wife, my friend, Robert, and my wife's classmate, Felicia. It happened on a Sunday morning and knowing that the problem wasn't going to be an easy fix, I asked my companions to continue their journey in a public transport, while I stayed to do whatever was necessary.

My wife was pregnant with our second daughter, Ozioma. She looked at me as to say, how we are going without you? I reassured her I would be okay without knowing if I was going to be safe or not. I ended up spending two days and two nights in the lonely, dry, and dusty road, working tirelessly with a half-baked roadside mechanic. In fact, I became an instant mechanic all through the process. I helped to make sure I didn't have to stay one minute longer than necessary.

The inconveniences and frustration from my car, the multiple three-hour trips to and from Kaduna for spare parts, and then hunger and thirst that hammered me were nothing compared to the mosquito bites I suffered in the two long and unending days and nights I spent there.

The mechanic was kind enough to surrender his bed to me. But he had no other place to sleep than the un-cemented oily and dusty floor of the batcher.

The bed had mattress that was made of grass. I thought it was good only if one wanted a body massage. On the bed were a pillow and a cover which was supposedly white, but visibly covered in dark patches of circular formation like a three-year old and some over night drools.

I could smell the stench of the pillow from the door. It was unbearable, but I had absolutely no choice. I contemplated on sleeping in my disabled car; it was risky to sleep outside.

The much I did to help myself was scatter my packet of cookie outside the batcher to keep rats and roaches busy and away from hunting on and around me. To make the situation worse, there was no restroom in the area. I used the nearby bush as my bathroom.

If I remembered it in time before night fell, I would have bought mosquito spray. It was a mistake I paid for dearly. If the battalion of mosquitoes fed on their usual victims one to three times at night, I guess they knew I was not going to be long and with my fresh blood, they eat me and had their reserves for the days to come. I also sensed they had some kind of underground network through which they invited their distant communities to feast on me.

When I was done with all the trouble on the car I was shaken in hunger, dehydrated, weak, and sleepy to my marrow. After driving off for about six miles, I stopped to buy gas and immediately a man stopped by me in his car and asked me to give his sister a ride to the East. I guess he knew where I came from through my car registration number. I agreed and asked the woman to get in the passenger's seat and off we went.

Within a few minutes I introduced myself to her and she did the same to me. With security at the back of my mind, I quickly asked if she needed to use the bathroom so that we won't have to stop anywhere for anything.

"No sir." She answered.

I asked this question because I have heard stories of people whose cars were snatched from them through women that pretended to be in need of car rides.

According to the stories, the women would purposely throw their head ties or handkerchiefs out the window at a prearranged location where the car snatchers lay in wait.

I was convinced I was too smart to lose my car in that silly way. I went everywhere with my eyes and mind open against anything that could have led me to lose my focus and my family car, the pride of a young married couple.

Conversely, I think my passenger needed me for the free ride as much as I needed her for company to dispel my sleep. If I survived it, I thought she was God-sent.

I did not sense any drama, yet I did not cease from expecting drama at every given moment, but if anything happened, it would take a Berlin Wall to stop me from escape. I was as ready as ready could be for any eventuality.

We had wide range of conversations: where she came from, married or single and so on. I told her I would like us to be friends, but not immediately, but in about six to twelve months down the road. I said it to occupy her mind and to suspend her knowledge about who I was. So I said to her, before the end of our trip I would tell her who I was and that she would be very surprised the person she was riding with. I was still flopping in my feeling between danger and safety of my car.

She gently reacted to my suggestion and asked why that far. And I said to her, "A good and lasting relationship is not likely to be picked up off the highway and if it is, should be well thought of, desired, and accepted without any rush."

At this point, I was satisfied I convinced her about starting a lasting relationship. Yet, I was to choose between two evils: to continue the journey through the night or find a place to sleep at Onitsha.

The time was 8:45 p.m. and the police check was in place on Onitsha Owerri road. The presence of the police was, without a doubt, a warning that danger was around the corner. So I stopped to ask the police a good place that we could check in for the night and they pointed to the social club hotel.

In two minutes we were there. As I contemplated on what to do with the young woman, I figured, she too was hesitant to check in with me. Her pause and the change of her demeanor were to me a positive signs that she might be genuine so I could rest my fears. She was ready to sleep in my car while I checked in to sleep in the hotel.

But my car was my biggest concern, not any other thing, not money, because I had spent every penny I had on the car.

If I left her in my car, I would have taken a terrible chance.

Though I had my pedal locks on, yet it wasn't a guarantee. I had already tempted the devil, riding with a stranger, stretching my luck to the limits. Taking another immediate risk would be irrational. Then, if I abandoned her, the brother, who put her in my car, could have gotten my registration number and if she got missing the police would be looking for me. And I would have questions to answer. It was a difficult situation.

I came up with an idea to have her stay with the receptionist, whom I paid some money to have her sleep on the floor behind the counter; and she did.

That was a big relief of the century for me, Thank God. Then and only then my brain started receiving adequate oxygen again and I felt as free as the desert air.

"Good lady, I do not mean you harm both of us are here for safety." Then I told her the sleeping arrangement that will dispel our fears of each other.

The night was quite and I slept like a log of wood and about 5 a.m I was up and at exactly 05:35 a.m. I went out to the reception to get her up and we left heading further southeast to Owerri.

Circumstances around us are not for us to loose, but to win, and win big in all fields of endeavors. I feel very good I won, but that was not without torment.

When I dropped her off at Owerri we wished each other safe trip without any attachments, no address requests, nothing.

Was what I did commendable, and given a chance would I do it again? In my judgment I think I was as close to death as shoes are to the soil. The thought of the incident brings recurring chills to my body. This is a warning: Be careful with strangers, because not everyone might be as lucky as I was. It doesn't matter how awfully near to the gates of decency and integrity; it's a jungle out there.

In my father's own words he said, "Stand for your principles even if you stand alone. Be there when people need you. Be devoted to your wife and be dedicated to your children. Flow with the stream. Be of service to your community in times of need, and have courage when things go wrong."

I didn't do the introduction I promised her and I hid the part of me that I was married with a child and had a second one on the way. It all came down to managing my composure for having a stranger in my family car, which, if I lost though carelessness, would be both unforgettable as well as an unforgivable act.

What bothered me most was what I would tell my wife if anything happened to our car. As it's rightly said, wherever your treasure is, there lies your heart. Mine was in my family car that was the biggest treasure to the family.

All my elements of reasoning and judgments were wide awake and burning in protection of our car anywhere I went.

We bought our cars in Africa with cash, no credit cards. Our checks would be refused unless the buyer is willing to wait until the car dealer or the owner goes to cash the check first before he releases the car to you. The weight of the cash and the number of years it took to work for it wasn't something you could repeat back to back without breaking your economic backbone.

Words matter: Life's a competition of the internal and external bodies, refereed by families, friends, and society.

We should coach our eyes, ears, and lips to benefit from the priceless life experience and tactic of others.

Life is a golden egg, worthy of replication. Don't destroy it. It is the single most precious gift we own.

While reading is a gift, writing shares one's creativity with the society and therefore is a blessing and a magnificent legacy of a lifetime.

Words matter we write to share. Words matter; write to educate and to be remembered.

No one has ever gone round the world, but writers do a thousand times over.

Chapter 14

Religion Belief and Practice

An Irish quote says: "I believe in the sun when it's not shining, I believe in love even when I feel it not, I believe in God even when he is silent."

Many things have been said about the business of cleansing of ourselves as we sit in prayers. What I do know is that when religious practice is used for public show, it ceases to serve our inner spiritual needs and then becomes public demonstration for earthly reward of self-image.

In my years of spiritual devotion in the seminary, we were never taught to act nor did we believe in acting in the name of the Holy Sprit coming down to speak in our tongues. To those who believe otherwise, I have asked the following substitute questions "Is speaking in tongue the real thing?"

Below are the model questions and the answers that I get.

(1) Q. Is God a deaf God?
     A. "No."
(2) Q. Does God understand all languages?
     A. "Yes."
(3) Q. Does God accept silent prayers?
     A. "Yes."

(4) Q. Is speaking in tongue a gift of the Holy Spirit and is it really a miracle?
A. "Yes, it's both spiritual and a miracle."
(5) Q. Do your members teach a new convert to speak in tongue and how?
A. "Yes, by teaching them the act."
(6) Q. An act?
(7) A. "Yes."
(8) Q. Who receives the miracle, the teacher or the student?
A. The student.
(9) Q. Is there any form of text that the student reads to aid remembering and understanding?
A. Yes.
(10) Q. Who would give the handout for study and memorization?
A. The pastor, one of our elders, or the teacher.

I am not a theologian, but in my knowledge of the Apostolic Creed I do not have vague relationship that shows the difference between originality and pretentiousness.

By definition, a teaching of any selection is an act of man not a divine gift of miracle.

A gift in the concept of religion has no connection with human teaching or learning. And religious practice should neither be deceitful nor made up. In all that I know, Christian religious practice is, should and must be the revelation and imitation of Christ, which should not be in conflict with foreign languages, accent, sexual uniqueness, or the color of our skin.

How true is tongue? Attestation: Paul, the apostle, downplays the importance of speaking in tongues. He said that he would rather speak 5 words that people can understand rather than 10,000 words in tongues. (1 Corinthians 14:14-19).

Speaking in Tongues appears again in Caesarea when Christianity was first taken to the Gentiles. (Acts 10:44-47).

The deception of speaking in tongue is awfully similar to the case of homosexuals; spreading the teaching of homosexuality in schools, as one of my interviewees said, if homosexuality isn't a choice, but genetic print; why teach it?

If it's a genetic print, obviously I personally do not have problems with what is real, but that, which is not.

Many people are turned off, confused, as they are with the gift of speaking in tongues.

Is it logistically apt, for anyone to go through the pain of learning and evoking a foreign or gibberish language while his audiences have no problems understanding the everyday language used in the shopping malls, in schools, and in football fields? We don't speak in tongue while watching basketball games or while eating our lunch and dinner.

Why would any one take the pain over what is free, speaking the same language, instead of tongue as renamed? But the tong business, as the scripture discloses is for "People from other lands" so that the listeners may understand.

It's such a showing off—pretending to be what one is not.

It's egotism, insensitivity—lack of consideration for others.

It's shameless and deliberate sham under the guides of religion.

It earns the architects earthly admiration without heavenly reward.

If we believe in what we say and swear to what we do in graciousness, no language should outshine or override another in the guise of tongues. It is deceitful, therefore to make people believe and to practice the heavenly gift of tongue.

Some years ago, in Nigeria, a bishop sent a multilingual Catholic priest for a psychiatric evaluation because the priest started celebrating masses, using about four or more of the languages he studied in the path of his education, and so claimed that he had the gift of the tongue including the power to expel demons.

Fundamentally, we understand "gift", not as what you worked for, but as a surprise package from someone, either for our birthday, wedding, Christmas or the like. We should not use people's claim of heavenly authority through rules of belief under the ignorance and innocent followers.

There was growing cynicism of sorts within the dioceses, where the priest served. In my sample test, question #5 above, it is simple conclusion that if the student received his gift of the tongue from the teacher, it means that the teacher – not the Holy Spirit – is the giver of the tongue. I do not know it all, but watch out for all kinds of garbage out there.

I affirm, for the sake of logical reasoning that if the needle of technology and the revolution of the world were dependent on such religious saga, we would simply be turning water into wine grass into petroleum, our bicycles into cargo planes, and the list can go on and on just at the flick of our fingers.

Today, anyone has the right to claim "Holier-than-thou" if he wants, but I disagree with the deliberate exaggeration about the meaning of a miracle. Never should fraud and hallucination be proclaimed as divine.

It bothers me more when grown men and women strap children's conscience with this kind of belief and have them go into the world in the handcuffs.

To further seal my point, mechanical prayer is a worldly overture equal to nothing. It only seeks secular rewards. Prayer is a spiritual communication between God and man, not a demonstration of funfair and for applause of men.

Let's see if we don't perceive anything wrong in this scenario; where a manager of a liquor store tells his staff to answer the phone and tell the caller that he is counting his money for immediate bank deposit. That is great risk.

As dangerous as it is to tell someone you have money for deposit, announcing you are praying causes immediate loss of your devotion. When we do so we make a holy impression of whom we want our addressee to think we are.

It is my analysis that as people would count their moneys in secret for their utmost security they should cut off their tongues in preservation of their religiousness.

If we do everything to secure our worldly wealth, we should do no less to secure our good judgment of prayer for our heavenly reward.

Our interface with God should not be a hot-air balloon. I don't have any problem with different denominations in religion, but with the individuals in all religions, whose characters, utterances, and behaviors are repugnant to reasonable range of societal standards. These people should find a part to the world.

Crucifix and other sacramentals are not deities of worship, but icons such as highway signs that offer directions to restaurants or gas stations. And in the case of restaurants and gas stations, it's your choice about what to eat or how much gas to buy.

Church buildings, mosques, and synagogues, whether built of gold or bamboo, may or may not sway one's spiritual attachment. What matters is the submission of one's body and mind to the will of God. Inanimate structures do not guarantee us heavenly reward either. What does is our love of God and our neighbors in the same way as we love ourselves.

A parent who routinely brushes his teeth every morning washes his hands with clean water and soap teaches the child the importance and the need for personal hygiene. This applies in all cases, including educating your child about how to react to any form of discrimination.

It doesn't matter whether you are tall or dumpy, success in school, games, and social engagements are the antidotes to discrimination. Success gives you confidence and comfort.

I admire President Obama and the great job his parents and grandparents did raising him. This leads me to the issue of racism. I am reminded of the situation of former Sen. Trent Lott of Mississippi, who made a racial comment Dec. 5, 2002, during the celebration of the 100th birthday of former Sen. Thurmond of South Carolina. Thurmond ran for president in 1948 and opposed civil rights polices. "I want to say this about my state," Lott said. "When Strom Thurmond ran for president, we voted for him. We're proud of it." "And if the rest of the country had followed our lead, we wouldn't have had all these problems over all these years either"(Associated Press Monday, December 9, 2002).

From time to time I tell my children racism is everywhere and that the one remedy against racial discrimination is excellence.

I read to my children a striking statement made by a White House official in the biography of Colin Powell. He, Jim Haskins said, "No one ever thinks of Colin as being black, they think of him as being good."

Regularly I charge my children not to come home with poor grades only to turn around and blame it on discrimination. I tell them the excuse of discrimination these days is a defeatist approach to growing up.

Chapter 15

Fond Memories of Africa

From the Wonder Years television show we are told, memory is a way of holding onto the things you love, the things you are, and the things you never want to lose.

As a dual citizen of the United States and Nigeria, I am asked by Americans how long I have been here and when I am going back to Africa. Others ask, "Do you miss home?"

My answer is, "Of course I do miss home so badly words can not express.

And it's not just me—emigrants, from all parts of the world miss their homes, I emphasize.

Home for us, I reiterate, is for the most part not only about our surroundings, no matter how grungy, it constantly changes as with all places. It's about the memory of our early childhood friends at school, church activities, and out-of-school games that habitually snowed under our childhood virtues.

We never needed any sweetener to enjoy whatever came our way. We didn't concern ourselves with adult matters and that's the way it still is with all kids.

Everyone of us considered intelligent, responsible things were for adults only, in the same way as going to vote in any election. It means nothing to kids if the elections went one way or the other. We lived in our own world.

We couldn't help ourselves to be better children no matter how much we tried to be "children of God," particularly in the way our daily catechism prescribed.

We were very good in reciting our catechism which made our teachers feel good about us. We did well in our religious knowledge competition which I think didn't reflect on our expected moral fiber. It could be we needed closer supervision to go along with our catechism classes which could have prevented us from being naughty children we were told we were.

I think all of us remember those childhood days so much that we desire to wind the clock backwards, to dig up those priceless memories to see if we could have done anything differently, wishing for a second chance. Edward de Bono, author, "How to Have a Beautiful Mind" wrote: "A memory is what is left when something happens and does not completely unhappen." The bad side—the gloomy part of the memories of my home is when I get the news that any of my childhood friends has passed away. Each time that happens, I overtly loose a part of myself.

I immigrated not thinking that I would return not to meet all my friends alive and healthy. So far nature has not been patient with me.

I thought there could have been a time when all of us, schoolmates and playmates would sit down collectively around a dinner table to eat, drink, and share the common stories of our growing-up. For example, we were able to escape from the watch of our parents, who kept us from mischief and then the unfriendly conditions of our time. In those days when our health was perpetually under the mercy of: mosquitoes, malaria, jaundice, measles, smallpox, and hookworms from the infected food we ate and the water we drank without any idea of basic hygiene.

We didn't know there were classifications of good and bad drinking water. We drank water from every nearby yellowish pound, but didn't die. We fanned off oversize latrine fries from our moldy mangoes and ate them without washing them and still made it alive. We fell from treetops, broke our arms and legs, yet hid them from our parents for fear they would be angry with us. We thought if we were stopped from our innermost activities with our peers it might take away the stockpile of joy in our heart.

We childishly plaid with every conceivable danger to the beam of death and still got free. To sum it up, I believe our guardian Angels were at home with us; thank goodness they didn't have a second job!

I miss my mother so badly and regret I can't help her in her old age.

There are no nursing homes or old people's homes, in almost all parts of Africa, where I would have kept Mom for better care.

She regularly suffers from dehydration and malnutrition not because we do not have enough food and fluid available for her, but because the woman employed to take care of her is without supervision and so chooses to nourish herself instead of my Mom. It's tough to deal with such a situation especially when you are about 8,000 miles from home.

From such a distance between the continents of Africa and North America, I dream of the typical village in which I was born and raised. I remember the locations of those trees that I had fun climbing.

I think of those mango trees that helped polish my climbing skills and also gave me the first taste of natural syrup that was not meant for my tropical malarial fiver or dry cough remedies. I would like to go home and touch those trees and hug them one after the other, if possible kiss them on their rough and worn out trunks for they must have grown taller and older than what my imagination has in print.

Maybe they will remember me from the time when I was young and they were smaller, tender, and brittle in their branches from where I tumbled and fail on my right knee at one instance and left shoulder at another.

Falling from the trees I violently buried some grasses under the soil. Instead of punishing me, the trees whistled me off the ground. "We don't mean to hurt you, buddy, be careful and come again," the trees might have whispered to me.

I would kiss and say to the trees, "hay, partners; I miss you so dearly and I thank you for being so sweet, kind, and loving trees."

In case the trees are dead by the time of my visit, and have their descendants by their sides, I would let them know how good their parent trees were to me and what good times we had together. I would show them my third-grade hand-drawn photographs of me hanging loose on their parents' branches and tell them what great risks I took before my childhood expired in my age.

But if the trees are dead without offspring, it will be my pleasure to look for the exact species of the trees that not only permitted me to be their playmates, but guaranteed me their generous juices and had my innocent life in their protection at the time that I was naive of the risks out-of-control children of my age had to face.

For watching over my back, I would not allow the trees to be extinct. I would replace the plants with rich soil and manure so that they would grow healthy and flourish for amazing outdoor activities of the present generation, who would fall in love with them and later have something good to say about them, in the same way I have done. This way a circle of regeneration will ensure that the present and the next, if they migrated to other countries will have one indisputable reason to visit their fatherland.

And to the soil, my incantation to them: For protecting my fragile knee and my shoulder from giving-up on me I would say: "Hey, mother earth, it doesn't matter how much you've been washed off by all the agents of denudation—rain, wind, wave, and animals, there are traces of my fingerprints within your crevices that link me to your habitat. Here I am, back to sing your praises after thinking of you for many years and realizing that good soil is as good as gold and for the favor, I thank you. I would be thankful that instead of throwing me six feet below, she put me up more than an inch above him.

Also it will be fun to recheck my skimming skill, running from our house to the mission to find out how far behind I have fallen in my speed. I would also like to test my courage in defying the darkness of the night. It's likely I might encounter night prowlers, who are constantly harassing the community these days.

Above all, I miss walking around my father's grave to connect with the more intimate memories of his sacrifices for me. It was his message and his approach to documentations that inspired my fiery interest in writing this book.

"Mel, it does not matter how busy you are and the power of your memory, record keeping will always be your best friend." He said that to me one day after his ugly experience with his kinsman, who accused him of holding back part of the money, he, my Dad kept for him. My dad was his community's banker at the time. Not knowing Dad kept detailed accounts of all his transactions, his accuser was defeated in his arguments.

I grew up in a very large and extended family, where we played together, and had great fun eating a mixed diet from our four different household kitchens. My first cousin, Caroline was active in making sure that I fed very well. She was the one who gave me the basic advice on sex education that I could not have gotten elsewhere. She introduced me to her girlfriends, whom I admired very much, but could not express my affinity to them. I was shy.

I guess one of them told her that which made her confront me one day and said, "Mel, someone is dying for you and not happy with you …."

"Who could that someone be and why was she, not happy with me?" I asked but she wouldn't say.

More than any other thing in the world, I liked to show off with my cousins, Caroline, and Euna and I guess our togetherness was one of the reasons that our family became a magnet to many young boys and girls of our age.

Every one of them wanted to identify himself or her self with us. To say it all, we shrilled and lit up the sky wherever we set foot. Huh! We were happy youngsters with our heads fixed in the clouds.

I was a rambler and didn't care about food that much. To make sure that I didn't starve, Caroline made sure that I eat my lunch and dinner with her. She wouldn't eat hers until I came home to share it with her.

Throughout the three years of war, Caroline occupied herself with varieties of novels and many of them were American detective magazines.

Being always in and out of the house—extremely boisterous, I missed the opportunity of the free time that I could have used to capture the early talent in omnivorous reading. It certainly would have improved my reading speed and better understanding. It is true life gives us brief moments with one another, yet in those brief moments we flash back on the memories that last a life time.

Just like typing, if you miss it at a tender age, it won't be over with you but to achieve speed in typing, no matter how much you try becomes a daunting task. I therefore do not doubt that reality of lost opportunities doesn't show favoritism—it sets in, and I was one heck of a victim of it.

Chapter 16

The Harvest of Habit

"All human actions have one or more of these seven causes: chance, nature, compulsions, habit, reason, passion and desire." (Aristotle, Ancient Greek Philosopher).

St Jude's primary school and uncle Cajatan's convenient store at the corner of the Mission served as our social and also our household point of attraction. The two places were our first-class flavor that answered our childhood needs by day and night.

My uncle's shop was about a mile from our house. It had most of the basic household essentials, especially kerosene and matches, bread, sugar, milk and tea.

As a child, I was so restive, forgetful, and undependable. I remembered nothing about anything no matter how seriously and important anything was. But one thing I never forgot was the treasure of hanging out with my group in our little world of no regret.

Maybe it was part of growing up that perhaps didn't go well with my father, but I now realize that most of the things that shaped me to who I am today were ties to those undeniable days of freedom I had together with my friends.

My father routinely left home very early each morning and returned home late in the evening. Most of the time he exploded in distress that we didn't have matches or kerosene for the nights, and would be mad at me in particular because he had given me the responsibility to make sure we didn't lack the two things in the house every night.

Out of 365 days in the year, I was expected to keep his need for kerosene and matches in view, but I had only Feast of St. Jude, Christmas, and the New Year dates in mind. The rest promised very little to me and to the other children of my age. So, we cared less about every other thing around us, but were devoted to remembering everything and doing things right at the approach of the three festive calendar days in addition to the ester.

Flashlights were more portable and guaranteed; it would have been less strenuous on my shoulders and frustration-free if my dad owned a flashlight and a pair of batteries, instead of his bulky lantern, which always put me into trouble.

The canopy of the tropical trees on our way to the provision store through the mission square made it fearfully difficult for my younger brother, Ike or any other boy or girl to run errands to the store when Dad usually came home to shower, dine and relax.

My brother hardly ever kept pace with me and sometimes I played scary hide-and-seek on him in those thick blankets of darkness. I would speed far ahead of him and lay flat on the ground only to whoop at his back, a few inches off his ears.

I thought that was a cool. He cried his heart out, and without pause reported me to Mom and Dad. Even after his complaints, I never stopped frightening him because I was never afraid, and I wondered why anyone would be afraid when fear itself wasn't fearful of us.

At the time, in the early 1960s, we were told electricity was about 150 miles away from us in a small city of Enugu, the state capital of the Eastern Region then.

In those days, nights were thicker, darker, and appeared as solid objects, like ridges of mountains, stretching from the tall heavens down to our feet. I used the little narrow and snake-like cracks in between the canopy and the hidden sky over my head to figure out where the roads and the erosion holes were.

Today the image is quite different—the forests are largely diminished, and electricity, though irregular, now dwells in the countryside. And for that reason there's less demand for kerosene. If I grew up at the present time there would be no pressure on me for kerosene, which means that I would miss running as the desert misses rain.

Ike later withdrew from doing the late-evening runs with me to the mission and that helped to sharpen my feet, running without stopping all alone at the tempo of light. So, I trained myself for speed and took the talent through St. Jude's elementary school in Amuzi, St Mary's Minor Seminary in Orlu, and St. Peter Cleaver's Seminary in Opala.

I was so quick on my feet that our trainer, Mr. Heinz, a British missionary, who also taught us English gave me the nickname "A shot from a Gun." I ran with the name and a lot faster than he and I ever thought.

I represented my school in various track competitions and won countless prices of T-shirts, metal and rubber buckets, towels, blankets, and so on and I could count on Jude and his aggressive cheers from the start to the end.

It's possible I and a few others of my counterparts could have qualified for the Olympics competition if our school was not focused on our one-way journey toward priesthood.

Running, for me, is a supreme outdoor exercise that I have great fun doing. I show my absorption in running at any given opportunity; sometimes competing with my children and beating them too. According to Jim Rohn, an American speaker and author, "Excellence is not a singular act, but a habit. You are what you repeatedly do."

Sometimes, when I go to the mall alone for shopping, I will park my car at the furthermost parking space so that I can run the entire span of the car lot, into the mall, and out, when I'm done shopping.

Here, American men, women, and children run to keep healthy. Up to this date, it is difficult for me to resist the magnetic obsession to join a race anywhere and at any time.

Sometimes, when I would be in different states, I would park my car and join any race along my path. I run not that I'm conscious of keeping fit, I run for the love of the habit. That reminds me: When Michael Jordan of the Chicago Bulls basketball team retired and came back the second time to play, he told the media he was back, not for the money, but the love of the game. I run for the love of the long ties to my passion that has been a part of who I am.

Everyone around me notices I don't walk the stairs; I run through them and simply can't stop running. I believe it will live with me as much as I'll live in it for a long time.

While I admire couples walking side by side into churches and walking trails, joining hands in leisure, I sympathize with my wife, who some of the time can't keep to my pace or have me join hands with her as others.

When I realize I'm way ahead of her, which usually comes with an apology, she says, "How many times would you do this?

I eat and drink fast too, and would not be sensitive of it till I hiccup.

As a phlebotomist, I worked with Denton Regional Medical Center, an ideal background for my quickness from the first floor, through the sixth and back to the laboratory. I never got to my destination unnoticed by fellow health-care workers and possibly patients' relatives, who might have commented about it in one way or the other.

Whenever we had 'code blue,' unless I was with a patient, I would answer the call in a flash of a second to obtain or provide whatever the doctors ordered. I realized it was all about life-saving. So if I ran going into the mall, I did no less in saving the lives of my patients.

One day, a nurse met me at the foot of the elevator and asked me if I was in the military. I didn't know why she asked me the question. So, as a matter of courtesy, I smiled and asked her why.

She smiled back and said she had tried to keep pace with me, but couldn't.

"You're not alone my wife complains too," I replied.

"What marvels me," she said, "is the razor-sharp twist you make at the corners as though you had your skating shoes on."

"It's out of many years of practice, nurse," I added.

Anyway, it is difficult to overcome.

My garden is my second-biggest interest. My vegetable garden is my gold. The times and attention I spend in the small piece of land in our backyard have been largely rewarding and I would like everyone to do the same, especially in hard times like we all have now.

I have been composting for a long time, even when I go to Chicago, Maryland and Las Vegas. I would bring my orange and banana peals home to my garden. Maybe people think I'm a neat-freak – and I am.

My parents taught me the importance of peasant-like cultivation of vegetables, pepper, okra and tomatoes. We were asked to water them in the dry season. I observed my mother making various types of vegetable soup to be our staple food. And it was from that time; I'm convinced, I started paying attention to the nutritional values of vegetables.

Today, whereas my neighbors are busy with keeping their dogs and cats, I make the most of my pastime in producing a lot of okra, green amaranth, basil, tomatoes, waterleaf, as well as garden eggs.

I like cats and dogs, but can't combine their needs with my vegetable garden. They might mess them up. I didn't grow up having pet dogs and cats. My uncle, who owned several of them, never kept them inside; they were let alone to fend for themselves.

People say: "If you are going to Washington, bring a dog." President George W. Bush's dog bit a journalist's hand in Washington. And it reminds me exactly the big bite my uncle's dog swooped on my right leg many years ago. People need to tell dogs not to bite us for the favor to go around.

I bought a big freezer to accommodate the large produce of vegetables that we eat until the next planting season.

We Americans are yet to experience what austerity is all about. There are tremendous wastes in all our workplaces, especially in the healthcare industry and restaurants.

It's unimaginable how much homework that I have been able to do with scrap paper that would have been thrown into the garbage. I did much of my narratives and note-taken on the hundreds of pages of printing papers I picked in my office and made use of them when I was away from my computer.

I thought I was alone, in the "go-green" campaign, but I was astonished when Seble, my medical laboratory supervisor at the Texas Oncology, north campus in Denton showed me a drawer full of scrap papers and said, "Mel, see if you would make use of these."

She had seen me come in before the end of my lunch break, and as I was gazing—writing. She looked at me and asked, "Mel, what do you write all the time?"

I answered, "I am obsessed with writing infinite deal of nothing in the hope that one day something could stick on the wall and would find its way to the book shelf."

She was impressed with my dreams and then opened the drawer filled with scrap papers and said to me, "Mel, you help yourself with as many as you would; I have been saving these papers and thinking that maybe they could be of use someday."

I was encouraged more than ever to continue my writing in the hope that sooner than later I would show Seble my publication as one part of the product of her scrap-paper savings.

I write when I drop my wife at her salon. I write while in the airplane, in my hotel rooms and, while in Africa, I observed and made my notes of informative things to share with the outside world. I wrote on scrap papers when my laptop would be out of power and couldn't get it recharged because the National Power Authority in Nigeria was undesirably inefficient, which earned her the nickname: Never Expect Power Always.

There were a few situations in which NEPA could be depended on for power, such as during the world soccer competitions and the U.S. presidential election.

As far as world soccer and the United States politics go, you could feel the passion of the events all across the continent of Africa—from Cape Town, to Cape Verde, from Morocco, to Madagascar, Egypt to the Republic of Zaire, also from Mali to Somalia.

With more dynamic focus from Nigeria, private and government offices across the nation turned off their assignments and then tune in for the events. Market places in Kano, Kaduna, Aba, Onitsha, through Lagos—ASPAMDA, and Alaba International Market, take a brake in market activities for soccer and the U.S. elections.

That is the culture in Africa, where all their eyes are on the U.S. You may ask just about anyone.

I continued writing and hoping that sometime it would be useful in the same way my supervisor thought of her saved scrap papers. Nothing surpasses the need for one to be ready for an opportunity.

In restaurants and in cafeterias, I always see people buy more food than they can eat and throw the rest away. It's a lot of waste I have seriously thought about why livestock and poultry owners don't go from one restaurant to another picking up the colossal waste of food and using them for their farms, instead of buying the expensive livestock and poultry feeds.

Their overhead costs would surely be lower and trickle down to consumers' advantage. If restaurants spend less on their meat products, they are more likely to thrive than close down for lack of profit, which translates to loss of jobs and loss of wages.

There is nothing in any journal, neither in the sky, nor in any school of thought that suggests that America is not uncivilized.

In the same journal, off the sky, or school of thought, nothing suggests that wasting of food is one of the elements and characteristics of a civilized society.

Why, then, do we waste food? It's high time we all learn about waste in restaurants, schools, hospitals, cafeterias and especially in all-you-can-eat buffets, which should be called all-you-can-waste buffets.

I had to teach my children – through my son, Udodi – about not wasting food. One day he threw a piece of meat in the garbage. I secretly sank it to the bottom of the trash and cut a new piece of meat to the same size and shape as the old piece. I put it on his plate and asked him to eat it.

Udodi ate it with bad feeling with his eyes closed; he thought he had eaten out of the garbage can and never knew the trick to this day.

He would know it for the first time, reading this book, that I actually didn't make him eat from the trash, but made him feel that way in order to discourage him from throwing food away.

In growing vegetables, I have also made a couple of hundreds of dollars selling the excess quantity my freezer could not hold. So, my 98 sq. ft. garden has helped me pay some portion of my water bills.

I have visited several countries and have seen waste of resources in the United States of America a trillion times more than any other places in the world. The campaign for saving the earth from peril may not be gathering enough steam, but the economic strangulation is the one enigma that can change our attitude.

For example, at the time a gallon of gas was less than $1.00 people would overfill their tanks to the extent that they waste about half pint of gas in overflow and it didn't bother anyone.

By the time the price of gas was over $4.00 per gallon, Americans of all ages were seen religiously shaking in the last drop of the gas that is in the rubber hose and within the hub of the gas nozzle. I took about half a dozen photos of this reference.

Nowadays, people have reduced the number of electric bulbs in their bathrooms and hallways. Outside of our own house, in the front and at the back, birds have built their nests over and around the night lamps because we no longer switch on the security lights in order to save energy bills. Our window blinds are open to let in daylight to save electricity.

For each of our three full bathrooms, I bought several plastic buckets in which I asked every member of my family to save the initial cold water that runs out of the faucets when the tap is turned on in the shower or bathtub.

We are a family of six and because every one of us showers at different times of the day, we could save at least 12 gallons of water every day. And sometimes, especially in summer, when all of us take our shower two times daily in order to ward off the summer heat and hydrate our bodies, we save even more water.

My point of saving the water is to aid in watering our shrubs, trees, flowers, and grasses. The practice saves money and enhances the looks of our yard with flowery surrounding.

Initially, my wife thought my method of water conservation was excessively mechanical, debilitating, and time- consuming, and therefore was unenthusiastic to join me in the water-saving scheme.

I also flush the toilet and repeatedly do our laundry with the water we save.

Back in my garden, my vegetables enjoyed a tropical-rain-forest type of precipitation. Their leaves widened twice their regular sizes. Their greenness spoke a million words, and their yields overwhelmingly tripled.

One other good thing I did was go to a nearby gas station regularly for gallons of expired milk to benefit my little garden and flowers. Initially the store attendants refused me. They thought I was going to drink expired milk and feared I could put them in trouble if I got sick. To convince them, I had my wife take photographs of me watering the garden from a gallon of milk. When they saw the photographs, they showed interest in what I would do with their waste. If I didn't come in a couple of days, they would call me for a pickup, sometimes half a dozen or more gallons. I think it is one innovation worthy of emulation.

Enthusiastically listening to our neighbors comment about how gorgeous our front yard looks, my wife then joined in the water-saving scheme and then exceeded my expectations.

What she does is this: After saving the initial cold water of about a gallon in our bathroom she goes upstairs in our children's bathroom to fill up about two bucket of cold water. I gave the same orientation to my children but they wouldn't do it. The thought it was not worth the trouble. So we had enough water for our garden all the time, water that otherwise would have gone down the drains.

Each time I went into their bathrooms I would see that the rubber buckets which I asked them to use in saving water remain as empty as they were by the time I put them there. It might not be the same with all kids, but it makes you wonder whether they understand the concept of experiment and results.

During the rains, I line up plastic containers in the back yard to catch as much rain water as possible. Realizing how much our water bill went down and how far the rainwater was benefiting my vegetables, I expanded my idea by dragging our large recycling container to the backyard. I fill it up with rainwater.

With basic hygiene at the back of my mind, I made sure that I saved my vegetables from contaminated water.

About four to six days after Texas weather gets back to its usual dry and gusty condition, I would water my garden off the containers two times a day. As a result, my vegetables burnish in their leaves.

My point is this—it's not only within the federal and state recycling establishments that we should pay attention toward saving the Earth's for present and future generations.

We as individuals have ample opportunities all around us, in our homes, places of work, hospitals, and restaurants to revamp the planet, one spot at a time.

Chapter 17

Events and Adventures

"Do not go where the path may lead; go instead where there is no path and leave a trail." (Ralph Waldo Emerson, an American author, philosopher and a poet).

Like many other child, my pugnacious tendencies were a concern to my father so much that he tried to set me straight. In his desperate intention to recover me, he handed me out to a primary school teacher, Mr. Paul Steve (actual name withheld). He was one of the teachers at St. Jude's Primary School in Amuzi. He was a staunch disciplinarian and plucky educator, one whom my father thought would use his position and teaching skills to cut down on my debaucheries and put me through to my studies in place of fighting.

Unfortunately, my Dad's provisions for my overall rehabilitation failed. Behaviorally, I developed into a puzzle my master could not solve. The major problem was not just me but my playmates who would not stop making fun of me and kicking me at the same time. I had no choice than revenge. And for ever strike I received I liked to double or triple it to scare my attackers away. I can't tell how much it helped or worsened the situation.

My master was fed up with me and could have sent me on my way, but I believe he didn't want to miss the benefits of the free food supplies my father kept bringing at the beginning of each month.

On the other hand I was every teacher's boy, sent everywhere on errands that I carried out at the tip of my toes. Actually, as I reflect, I regret that the teachers used me as a tool on the premises. I was a willing horse, so every one of them overlabored me. Every one of them reckoned on what I could do for him and none cared about the problem it was for my future, knowing that as a child, I needed the same help and true direction they give to their biological children. I thought it was an abuse and my patents did not know I was suffering in silence.

It wasn't fun cooking for everyone in the household while every other person enjoyed the endless advertisements and national news off a massive radio. I looked it up; the Grundig radio big box is costing $31.00 now, with free shipping, at that time no more than $5.00. My master happened to be one of the few teachers that were able to afford that kind of radio, thunderous in volume. Consequently, his house was crowded with other teachers at 7 p.m. daily for the national news headlines, and all of them listened to the rest of the news with exceptional attention.

Like hawks, they had either their right or left ears turned to the direction of the radio. The teachers and their wives would be looking at you without seeing you.

Not that the radio was not loud enough; you could hear it from about a mile away, especially during the harmattan, when the dusty, dry winds from the Sahara Desert give flight to the sounds and whistles along its path.

Habitually, I noticed that the teachers didn't tilt their heads when the news was read in the native vernacular, but they did when it was in English format.

Beside our parents, our teachers were our only role models, imitating them in the ways they walked, talked, joked, and laughed. Seeing them listen to the news in a particular position with their heads tilted, mouths agape, we emulated them in the presumption that it was an official pose for listening to the news.

Not until many years later did we realized that they were lacking in vocabulary for good comprehension of the news in English. Till today we have not stopped joking and laughing about it, especially when we see the hawks and other birds of the Earth looking up. It quickly reminds us of the good old days with our model teachers at St. Jude's Primary School.

The teachers' news time was our time—the house boys' time, our cherished free play when no one was watching. In their rapt attention to the British Broadcasting Corporation (BBC) of London or Voice of America (V.O.A.) we, the teachers' boys, evolved every mischief under our skin and got away with them in style.

Teachers cooked with firewood and their kitchens were quite a distance away from their apartments. The reason for this was to keep their rooms away from the smoke and the smudges discharged from the firewood of the kitchens. It is likely also that the early missionaries, who planned the teachers' quarters, knew the dangers of carbon monoxide way back when, and for that reason the kitchens were located away from the living areas. Not one of the kitchens had a door against dogs and other large animals that were attracted by the crumbs and droplets of food on the floor.

The first week of my cooking assignment was a nightmare. Rice was considered a special food, exclusive for the "rich," whatever measure of richness that was then. The teachers who could afford to eat rice once a week made their servants happier. They were happier with the effervescent smell of fried red palm oil and red onions that beclouded the atmosphere and persisted for a long time because the undulating canopies of the tropical rain forest vegetation had little gap for the intense odor to escape into the clouds.

Even if we didn't share in the food, we were satisfied with the smell and desired for it to hang around for ever. And what's more, we would do any errand in order to get a share of the rice, usually on our palms. If we are lucky to have a drop of the fry touch our palms, we would lick it till we went to bed. The scent remained there the next day and smelling it, we would be equally as satisfied as eating it. If we had anything to do in the rain we made sure we protected scent from being washed off.

In one occasion, as soon as I was done cooking rice, the woman of the house, came to take charge of the kitchen to fix the stew. When the sauce was ready, she would order me to carry the pot of rice to the leaving room while she came right behind me carrying the hot stew.

To make sure she insulated her hands from burning, she would slap two pieces of dry banana leaves or old news paper of West African Pilot or Daily Times to the opposite sides of the pot. The moment I put the pot of rice down, her second order was for me to get everyone's plate marshaled out on the floor of the living room.

Through my usual quickness of action, I carried out the order like a razor.

Without regret, the woman scratched just a spoon of rice into the plate my father bought for me.

Good for their dog, named Sandy, I wasted no time in throwing it to the dog, but she filled up the other children's plates to the rim. I sure wasn't there for the food.

At the beginning of every month, my father would bring in enough rice, beans, Geri, yam, and stockfish to help out with my feeding. Each month that my father brought us groceries, they thanked him dearly for his generosity and fed me well for that single day. But the rest of the remaining 29 days she turned around to starve me to my bones.

This experience might have contributed to my moderate eating habit to this day—perfect to my body metabolism, while others worry about how to cut down on their food consumption.

To deal with this situation I remembered what my grand father said, "You can't cross the ocean merely by standing and staring at the waters." I devised two ways of keeping my body and soul together. A boy as hyperactive as I was needed good nourishment to function, being everywhere at any time and at the speed of light too. In reference to my quickness, the difference between a spirit and me was like a tendril of a human hair. In the predicament, I called up my feet to the task, dashing into my family home, about a mile from the teachers' quarters, into my mother's kitchen, grabbing as much food as I could, and in exactly ten minutes I was back to the premises full and fulfilled for the day.

The second technique was less consuming. I formed the habit of eating my rice, beans, yam, or Gari without sauce before Mrs. Paul came into the kitchen. This was necessary because my mother, particularly, was getting concerned that I was starving in the teacher's house. My father was hardly at home, so unless he was told, he wouldn't know anything about my situation at all.

My procedure was simple: About five minutes before the rice was done, I would quickly scoop two big spoons of rice from the bottom of the pot, then mend the surface of the rice to equal level, and then sprinkle fresh water over it and put back the cover for the steam to level the surface. The moment I did this, I would show myself to her in anticipation of her question, "Mel, is the rice not cooked yet?"

"No ma, in about a few minutes," I would reply.

I didn't run back to the kitchen this time; otherwise I would attract attention and suspicion. I walked leisurely, picking up some firewood to create the impression that the cooking needed a little more steaming.

My purposeful delay, together with my uncoordinated whistling as I walked through, was for the mangled rice to shape up and for the scoop of rice I hid in a corner to cool off a bit for my tongue to handle. In this way, I learned to eat my rice fast without sauce and without flavor. It paid off.

Up to this day, I can eat my rice, beans or yam with little or no sauce at all. And to my greatest excitement, here in America today, many health journals advise against fried food because of cholesterol. Thank goodness, I don't miss fried food at all. It is truly another way in which I have benefited from my early childhood experience.

In another case, when people were mean-spirited to me, I protested by stirring the soup with a spoon or my fingers to make sure the soup became sourer by morning. That way it would be thrown away so that all of us, big and small would be deprived of it.

I called up this same trick against my cousins, Dominic, Leo, Kenneth, and Cashmere who made fun of me for eating cornmeal all the time, not knowing that I had reaction to the cyanic acid in cassava-gari, so that forced me not to eat the same stuff as they did.

At every opportunity, night or day, I made sure their soup was sourer. They suspected that I was the cause and wanted to catch me in the act, but I was smarter than that.

Children are comparable to liquefying iceberg, radical and risky; they can make some rough judgments out of flaming situations.

I am glad that my early childhood experience gave me the get-up-and-go and the know-how of the domestic routine that I bring into my daily live.

Chapter 18

Ticks of Politics 2008

If we don't take care of politics, politics will take care of us. After the failures of the 2000 and 2004 elections, Americans might have gotten it right in 2008.

We didn't have much blame in voting for George W. Bush in the 2000 presidential election despite the entire jumble of the Supreme Court Georges.

The much talked about experience we all consider to be key in running for the White House differed with Mr. Bush coming out with his experience as Governor of Texas. Many Americans believe we got into this big mess when not only did we see the entire handwriting on the wall but saw the walls fall, stepped on top of it and went ahead and voted president Bush the second time.

Soon after that America realized its mistake and started pointing fingers because violence continued to spiral in Iraq, three years after the US-led invasion. As a key architect of the war in Iraq, The defense secretary, Donald Rumsfeld had faced growing criticism and calls to step-down.

Senator John Rockefeller, senior Democrat on the Senate Intelligence Committee said, "Secretary Rumsfeld's war plans in Iraq have failed. The country is on a dangerous course, and the administration has finally recognised the need for drastic, immediate change."

When Mr. Rumsfeld was asked by a New York audience about connections between Saddam Hussein and Osama Bin Laden he answered, "To my knowledge, I have not seen any strong, hard evidence that links the two." news.bbc.co.uk/2/hi/americas/3715396. stm. America took note.

Dramatically, Mr. Rumsfeld issued a statement saying his comments had been "regrettably misunderstood" and that he had acknowledged there were ties between Osama Bin Laden and Iraq based upon CIA intelligence.

America saw clear evidence of flip-flopping and made up its mind, saying the case for the war was bungled.

The Observer stated, "Senior American officials concluded at the beginning of last May 2004 that there were no weapons of mass destruction (WMD) in Iraq.

Intelligence official who spoke on condition of anonymity, said they had enough evidence at the beginning of May, 2004 to start asking, "Where did we go wrong?" "We had already made the judgment that something very wrong had happened [in May] and our confidence was shaken to its foundations."

"Arizona Republican Senator John McCain broke party ranks to join Democratic demands for an independent probe into how US intelligence got it wrong, given the failure by searchers to find weapons of mass destruction."http://www.guardian.co.uk/world/2004/feb/01/usa.iraq

But BBC News website world affairs correspondent Paul Reynolds said, Mr. Rumsfeld resignation was a sign and an admission that the US policy in Iraq has not worked, so far.

Instead of following the trail of deception to vote against the war, the catholic authorities campaigned against Sen. John Kerry of Massachusetts on abortion.

I am a catholic, and I am also against abortion. War and abortion are deadly; we need not lean our support for one and treat the other with, "We don't care attitude." Both are evil.

I recall the United States Roman Catholic campaigned against Al Gore, but not as vigorously as they did in the case of John Kerry.

In election, we should vote our sense of right and wrong. But it does seem to me that the Catholic leadership is intolerant of a particular party and has her eye in favor of one party system of government if given a chance.

My analysis is this: If two football teams are playing a game, there's always a reason we like one team more than the other. Even in the particular team we support, we might like a player or a couple of them more than the others. It's fair judgment.

The Catholic community overwhelmingly voted for President George Bush, not a problem. But after seeing the "wonderful job" he did for the Nation and our standing in the world, I thought we the custodians of beliefs and morality should apologize not only to Sen. John Kerry, but to America as a whole. We can't be wrong and right at the same time.

We all have sense of right and wrong. In elections, everyone should vote his or her conscience rather than have any religious institution; Christians try to swear and influence our conscience from the podium of worship, using abortion as an excuse with exclusion of the war in Iraq. Again, we missed great opportunities by supporting out of political leanings.

Our faith doesn't make us inanimate or unresponsive to our surroundings and I am so glad that in this 2008 election, we stopped and looked before we voted. That's how it should be in a free society.

We should not reward failure. Thank goodness we didn't forget we weren't going to get a better result from same old players.

We know what sin is; in our Catholic dogma, abortion is forbidden. We do know also that war is profane as abortion; and I want us to preach and hear of the two: abortion and war—side by side to make sure we feed the goose as well as the gander. The Bible says, "Give to Caesar what is Caesar's, and to God, what is God's.

I would vote against a Democrat running the same type of Government as the Republican president did in the last eight years. That's being fair and that's what people of goodwill should be doing and preaching, not otherwise.

Here's my proof: If we, the Catholic family, were parents to Sen. Kerry, who has different view about abortion, would we cast him out of the family in support of our other son, who took the nation to war because, "After all, this is the guy who tried to kill my dad." Or some other political reason? You be the judge.

Don't you think the increase in the percentage of Catholic voters in 2008 is certainly a message—we should not fail to understand—a message of, "it's enough." So we collectively and politely said: "No, not this time …" which translated to 54 % of Catholic votes for President Obama.

I am such an independent thinker, not driven by the parties. If Barack's outcome of Government is similar to Bush, I will not see him differently; one strike, he's out, no second chance as was our collective mistake in the case of President Bush.

Other than the economic meltdown, the second and the third factors that sent Barack Obama to the White House were the issues of Reverend Jeremiah Wright. America refused to be blind-folded again—once beaten, twice shy.

First of all, America heard Reverend Wright's bombastic words, evaluated and dismissed them.

Obama's attempts in defending him as a good guy for the 20 years he knew him as his pastor didn't melt Wright's heart.

Then Senator McCain and his political machinery tried using Reverend Wright to improve their political vantage point with the question: "Who is the real Barack Obama?" Before now they campaign had planted a response to yell, "He is a Muslim!"

They claimed he was Muslim, and one to be feared, lacked merit. "I'm afraid of him," a woman uncomfortably stammered to McCain and then handed him over the microphone.

From another perspective, when Reverend Write wouldn't back down in his remarks, the American voting public was quick to realize that Wright was conscious of what he was doing, and there was whispering at every corner that he was obviously jealous of Obama's inspiring popularity, which was likely to send him to the White House.

The scrupulous American nation deliberated about Reverend Wright's actions and utterances in a variety of ways. Their question was: Would he, Reverend Wright, have instigated and unremittingly continued his offensive televised outbursts if Barack Obama was his son or brother—having come this far in the race to be president of the United States of America?

At that time, Reverend Wright should have called for calm in the sea, instead he invoked a tsunami. There were doubts that he wanted Obama to succeed and my beloved Americans, whites, blacks, gay, straight, Jews, Christians, Muslims, Republicans, Independents, and Democrats, everyone understood the negative message Reverend

Write had for Barack. When the public came to judgment, Barack's favorability went up to 69 percent.

McCain and Governor Palin continued scoring negative points each time they dwelled on the negative attacks, trawling for a good message and unfortunately, no, I meant, fortunately, to Obama's advantage.

For a second time, my analysis is that if Sen. McCain was much younger or a little closer to Barack Obama's age, the American voters would have considered the contest fair. Here's the catch, in both culture and folklore, there are things expected of elderly statesmen, for instance, what is expected of a grandparent to say or do and things he should not.

As an elderly statesman in the ring, McCain was punching below the belt. It was almost comparable to Mike Tyson biting off Evander Holyfield's right ear in the ring.

Americans called a foul on McCain and threw him out for making points that didn't make sense and for promoting fear, not hope.

If Sen. McCain could have swayed Sen. Hillary's Clinton's million supporters, he previously distorted Sen. Clinton's record on issues such as health care, taxes, the environment, and housing; he also issued several personal attacks against Clinton and her family.

His attacks were still too fresh in Hillary supporter's minds and so couldn't have sat well with them when he turned around, 360°, saying: "She has inspired generations of American women to believe that they can reach the highest office in this nation. And I respect her campaign, and I respect her." America responded by saying that McCain's flattery was noticeable as well as deceitful. They then decided not to go with him.

Another potential problem was Bill Ayers, an anti-Vietnam War group that protested U.S. policies by bombing the Pentagon, U.S. Capitol and a string of other government buildings. The FBI labeled him a "domestic terrorist.

When Senator McCain's used Barack's relationship to Bill Ayers to question Baracks patriotism, Mr. Ayer's silence gave a chilling bombshell to Senator McCain's campaign and the media too.

McCain's campaign couldn't hold Barack at anything new. Bill Ayers said absolutely nothing for or against Barack Obama, unlike Reverend Wright.

I am certain Bill understood that silence is a fence around wisdom and I personally thought that he, Ayers considered the time his name came up in the campaign as a period of reckoning, which turned out to be positive for him and for Barack Obama. The outcome of which, fits into William Wordsworth saying that *calm is all nature as a resting wheel*; and we could hear the footsteps of God when such silence reigns.

How nice it is to make my voice heard; even when I thought my voice wasn't going anywhere, and that no one was listening, I put my voice out and loud for Obama's campaign.

Although, at the start of the presidential election, I was in full support of Sen. Hillary Clinton for president. I, like many others thought Barack Obama was going to be one of those that would likely fall by the wayside. I also liked Sen. Joe. Biden, but I came head and shoulders in support of Sen. Clinton. The same day she announced her candidacy, I wrote:

Dear Sen. Hillary,

America loves you. Come be the mother of our nation so that America would be born again through your womb. Come fix our nation and bring our friends back to our fold ....

Yours truly,

Mel Igbokwe.

It didn't take long before I realized that voting for Sen. Hillary could send a wrong message to the third-world countries. They would, I thought, think American presidency is an exclusive concession to the few—a handover as it appears with President H. Bush to his son President George W. Bush, and then President Bill Clinton to the wife, Hillary Clinton. I don't support blindly; I weigh all the options to get a feel of where the cat was going to jump and whether it was jumping to safety.

Nothing on earth would convince the third world that the election wasn't a handover.

"It's a power handover," they would say, and their campaign slogan would be: "If it happened in America, it could elsewhere."

With all eyes on America, I panicked that the third-world politicians would, after the end of one person's term, manipulate the election results in favor of their sons, daughters, or their wives and defend it by suggesting that they are adopting the American archetype—from father to son, husband to wife, and so on.

Through this perception, I quickly made a U-turn, backing off Sen. Hillary Clinton in full support of Barack Obama, as Sen. Joe Biden was lacking in steam.

Having that courage of my conviction, I came out in full blast with ideas and suggestions, writing, e-mailing, and faxing my strategies to Obama's offices

In due course, I made it all the way to become one of Obama's pledged delegates, which I think gave my voice a little more attention.

For example, after Sen. Obama's second debate with Sen. McCain in Nashville on Oct. 7, 2008, I wrote:

Dear Campaign Manager
Obama for America

Attn: David,
Although Barack Obama did well in tonight's debate, he should have done much better.

In everything I know about debates, one doesn't allow his opponent to unleash any sticky word, statement or phrase as "Obama doesn't understand" against him without throwing back a comparative and superlative words or phrases, synonyms, or at least use the same expression to weaken his repetitive points.

McCain would have fled and dwelled on experience; but because of his running-mate, Gov. Palin, he spun away from experience platform to "Sen. Obama doesn't understand" recitation.

"Watch out, he's not done yet; Obama should wait for him in the next debate."

I would like him to respond thus: I understand more than you do, Senator, and all Americans understand why we should not have gone to war in Iraq, and John did not; instead he voted for the war.

Second, the effects are clear; John's policy with Bush has brought the economic meltdown. I understood why we almost not had this debate tonight; it's the failed policy of eight years, under your watch that brought you and I her today.

I understand foreclosure home is not a story tell; it is real and happening right now.

I understand what people, who have lost their jobs are going through. Students can not go to college because Banks are closing against their college loans.

I have listened to ordinary Americans whose wages have been overtaken by the inflection and don't have a voice in Washington to lift them up. If you understood that, you would have taken care of them than the wealthy you have supported their tax cuts in the last eight years.

What I don't understand really, is why you, McCain, still want to continue with the policies that have gotten us where we are today.

I don't think John remembers we had surplus in our hands 8 years ago, and voting 90% in support of Bush in every step of the way, the surplus vanished. I know better and every American understands why.

And it's for that 3 letter word, WHY, that I call for Change; a change to better Americans' future, at home and across the globe. John McCain does not get it; we must not build a wall against our enemies, it is civil to talk to them, it's civil to open our windows of oxygen for them to breathe as we educate them to choose peace, in place of war.

McCain may not understand that the Men and Women, who could have been better citizens; better Senators or perhaps better Presidents, have lost their lives in a war that should not have been waged or authorized. Senator McCain, where do you draw your moral judgment about the Iraq war?

Mel Igbokwe.
Pledged Delegate.

Happily, in their next debate, Sen. Obama did what Napoleon could not do by unleashing his response in the way that I and perhaps others suggested; I could hear my own remarks in his voice, which made McCain flee, as I thought, and then gave Barack the advantage to run away with victory. The outcome of the debate was dynamite.

I continued to write and fax many more letters as the election progressed. And when Sen. Obama secured the Democratic nomination, June 3 2008; fearing that it would be difficult for him to win the general election, I came back rebooting my skyrocketing interest in Hillary, asking desperately that Obama choose Sen. Clinton for his running mate.

To my greatest surprise, he didn't and that kind of numbed my concentration in the process. I panicked that Obama was inches from loosing an opportunity of a lifetime. And in my electronic mails to a friend overseas, I said I was going to be in prayer until Obama's success. I was shaken and sleepless.

"Could he win with a landslide," I asked myself? I thought—only if he had Hillary on his hip belt.

Winning without Hillary, I thought, Obama would have to work too hard to win the election, and would be terribly drained. I was still very much involved emotionally.

I tentatively embraced Obama's loss before it might happen so that I wouldn't have a sudden heart attack. I was restless about the election like no other I spent time watching, campaigning, writing, e-mailing, and one in which I donated to its success for the first time.

Then if any miracle happened in his favor, I prayed, my enthusiasm in the process would be reactivated.

I probably worried, prayed, and stayed awake more than some of the candidates. I only wished and hoped he would not slaughter the opportunity of his lifetime.

How else could a passionate supporter identify with a party and its candidate? I did it all and more.

I am, like many other Americans and the world, proud of the historic election. I kept my phone lines open with people in Nigeria and I listened to the sounds and music of semiautomatic weapons in Lagos, Imo State, and Abia state, honoring Obama's victory.

I also called my fiends and family in England and their yells of joy were loud enough to blow off their rooftops. My ears were throbbing from their shouts through telephone.

America sets the pace and drives the bus for the rest of the world to follow, and I am as happy as millions of others to be part of what has gone down in the history of my generation. We did it and will do it again. Next time it could be a woman we'll send to the White House.

Sometimes persuasion works better then imposition.

From the excerpt of The Tower newspaper of American University, Nov. 14, 2009, His Eminence James Francis Cardinal Stafford criticized President-elect Barack Obama as "aggressive, disruptive and apocalyptic," and said he campaigned on an "extremist anti-life platform."

I thought the Cardinal's point of view about Obama's style of campaign can also be viewed as unconvincing as it was silent on the war and the economy which were the major concerns of Americans.

We all have different views about everything and anything, up to our choices of food and fluids. I think we should not choose between war and abortion the two should be treated as two iniquities.

Chapter 19

The Apex of All Eyes on US

The summit: When history is made, as in the most recent one in the United States presidential election, there are pertinent notes and basic lessons we all should preserve as truthful, not fiction about what happened and how it all happened, which would be precious for generations to come.

If Mitt Romney, an equally, likable and charismatic 2008, Republican Presidential candidate won his party's nomination I would surely have voted for him.

On the other hand, Barack's choice of an "Attack-dog" in Sen. Joe Bidden, with mammoth domestic and foreign policy experiences couldn't be wiser. In their onetime vice-presidential debate, America made an on-the-spot assessment of Joe Bidden and Sarah Palin. They favored Bidden.

Govornor Palin of Alaska didn't fit into what McCain had said he would look for in his vice-president: "Ability to be president." His gamble to run with Palin was a surprise to many conservative republicans.

I couldn't agree more that the political caterpillar of the Republican Party—Newt Gingrich, was on vacation when McCain's political yacht was leaking and his single "Maverick" engine was out of fuel.

Sen. McCain and Gov. Palin tenuously captured national attention during their 4 day convention in Saint Paul Minneapolis, but their campaign took a nosedive after Palin's televised interviews with Katie Couric of CBS News.

Palin could not name a single News paper she reads, could not give her policy stand on the campaign finance crisis and example of Sen. McCain's vote for more regulation in both government and public sectors.

That was not all, Mrs. Palin had other problems looming over her qualification to be vice president to John McCain. She was a subject of an ethics investigate in Alaska, which claimed she had abused her official power.

The Judiciary found ample evidence of witch-hunting by Sarah Palin, that she used her power as governor to get her ex-brother-in-law forced out of job.

On one other side of the equation her "Hockey mom" personality was undermined by a disclosure that the Republican campaign spent $150,000 on her clothes and accessories at the time everyone in American was crying about the economy.

Then came the heavyweight Republican, Gen. Colin Powell's condemnation of the negative attacks on Sen. Barak Obama coming from the McCain campaign as having gone too far and according to Powell sowed increasing "narrowness" of his Republican party. He included that it was reason for his endorsement for Obama's candidacy; "Not because he's black."

As Barack was pounding away with his message of change, Mr. McCain could not fairly and easily find a sequence of message that worked. He stumbled from being a war hero, to the right to be heard long experience; from being a maverick, to giving temporary gas relief along with Mrs. Clinton, to a tax-cutter. Yet he never found a way to brighten up his star in the polls. He couldn't match the appeal of his articulate, captivating opponent. It was sorrowful to observe.

America saw Sen. McCain's abrupt suspension of his campaign to go back to Washington in other to fix the economic problem as artificial and misleading.

It seemed Obama's constant reminder for voters to watches out for utterances by his opponent to get by the election and then switch back to the same old policy when the election was over, no doubt resonated and paid off.

John McCain found himself bogged down in the middle of the throbbing economy and his quotes about the fundamentals of the economy being strong—documented in video tapes and released at the nick of time came back to haunt him.

According to BBC news his tax plan to favor the wealthy rang hollow with people facing foreclosure and job losses.

An additional troubling issue for McCain was his campaign funds. As Barack sat on huge comfortable public donation of over $650m, John McCain accepted the old method of federal funding which Obama out rightly rejected.

For this reason, he could not come close to Obama's ability in dominating the television airwaves, which translated to gaining Obama many traditionally Republican strong hold, namely: Colorado, Florida, Indiana, Iowa, New Mexico, Virginia, Nevada, and Ohio.

As a mostly loyal Republican, Sen. McCain's record was one of 98% support for President George W. Bush, which Barack Obama continued to bring up from sunrise to sundown.

McCain could not run away from his shadow. At one point Barack reminded voters that George W. Bush has dug a big hole for us and was handing his shovel to John McCain.

The visual image of the shovel couldn't be more forthcoming and for that Americans held the portrait of the shovel in mind and voted frustratingly and infuriatingly against the shovel.

Then came Oprah Winfrey's effect, who threw her support behind Sen. Barack Obama in the early stages of the campaign. Her support entrenched the seasoning that made Obama's White House dish delicious.

The CNN's Jason Carroll, commented about Oprah's impact on the polls as favorable.

In her CNN interview with Mr. Larry King about what made her endorse a candidate for the first time in her life. The talk show icon, Ms. Oprah Winfrey replied: "Because I know him (Barack) personally," "I think that what he stands for, what he has proven that he can stand for, what he has shown was worth me going out on a limb for – and I haven't done it in the past because I haven't felt that anybody, I didn't know anybody well enough to be able to say, I believe in this person."

Whereas Obama's favorability was punching the sky, Tina Fey's impersonation of Sarah Palin was at play with national ridicule. And Obama was seen off-limits for any legitimate bashing as it would have been alleged to be racially motivated.

After the election, we saw showers of many world leaders hailing the election of Senator Barack Obama as the first black president of the United States.

Gordon Brown, the United Kingdom Prime Minister said the American Election was historic and added that he "share many values" with Barack Obama.

The BBC's newscaster, Justin Webb in Washington DC said that Americans have made two deep-seated statements about themselves— that we are profoundly unhappy with the status quo, and that we are slamming the door on the country's racial past.

Behind that was the United Nation's Secretary General Ban Ki-moon, who declared that he was looking forwards "to an era of renewed partnership and a new multilateralism".

The Chinese President Hu Jintao said he looked forward to strengthening dialogue; while France's Nicolas Sarkozy said that the opinion poll had raised "enormous hope".

The Iranian President Mahmoud Ahmadinejad said that Iran is ready to attend talks with the United States on equal footing that is based on mutual respect.

The Egyptian President, Hosni Mubarak sent a congratulatory cable to Barack Obama following his victory in the election and stated in his message that he hopes Obama would help bring about peace and stability in the Middle East.

The Australian Prime Minister, Kevin Rudd, quoted: "Forty-five years ago Martin Luther King had a dream of an America where men and women would be judged not on the colour of their skin but on the content of their character, today what America has done is turn that dream into a reality," He concluded.

European nations applauded Mr Obama's victory and expressed hope that it would lead to a "new deal" and energize relations that has been strained after the US-led invasion of Iraq five years ago and eight years of the Bush Administration.

"By choosing you, the American people have chosen change, openness and optimism," President Sarkozy of France wrote in his letter to Mr Obama, praising him for a "brilliant victory" and astute electoral campaign. "At a time when all of us must face huge challenges together, your election raises great hope in France, in Europe and elsewhere in the world."

In Berlin's Unter den Linden Boulevard, where 200,000 people gathered to welcome Barack Obama in summer of 2008 at the hit of his bid to the White House, his admirers came out again in full strength to watch the election. The German Chancellor, Angela Merkel congratulated him on his "historic victory" and immediately extended another invitation to Obama. She said, "Be assured that my government is fully aware of the importance and of the worth of our transatlantic partnership."

Sometimes dire wishes can turn out to be an advantage as in the case of the Australian Prime minister, Mr John Howard's stinging attack on Barack Obama, just one day after Barack announced his candidacy to run for the White House and declared that, if elected, he would withdraw all US troops from Iraq by March 2008. "I think that would just encourage those who wanted completely to destabilize and destroy Iraq, and create chaos and victory for the terrorists to hang on and hope for an Obama victory," said Mr Howard. And he continued, "If I was running al Qaeda in Iraq, I would put a circle around March 2008, and pray, as many times as possible, for a victory not only for Obama, but also for the Democrats."

As much as we, the people of the United States enjoy world recognition, support, and alliances, we don't like any world leader to dictate for us what to do, whom we should or should not vote for in our elections; we see it as insult to our self-governing nation.

I wouldn't be effusive; I rather be calm and calculative as a leader of my country in matters concerning foreign politics and no other time would this be central than during transitional period of governments. It could make one look stupid and withdrawn thereafter, if the election didn't tilt to the party that one supports.

In Kenya, Obama's fatherland, the President, Mwai Kibaki declared a national holiday to celebrate Barack's victory.

Not unexpected is the voice from Rome, Pope Benedict XVI with the tradition of paying very close attention to the United States politics, unleashed his prayer for the New US president. "He assured Obama of his prayers that God would help him with his high responsibilities for his country and for the international community."

The Vatican spokes person, Father Lombardi said. The Pope had also prayed that, "the blessing of God would sustain him and the American people so that with all people of good will they could build a world of peace, solidarity and justice". It was reported that this message was sent through Mary Ann Glendon, the US ambassador to the Holy See.

Surprisingly, I observed a dislocation of tone that is in direct contrast with some U.S. Roman Catholic leaders, who have criticized its members for voting in large numbers in favor of Democrats.

Weighing the two positions, anyone would wonder why there is a departure in principle and practice within the hierarchy in Rome and its commissioners in the United States.

Bill Bradley, the retired NBA Basketball player said, "The only way to be true to our American tradition is to maintain absolute governmental neutrality regarding religious beliefs and practices."

Regarding the mix messages, I imagine the situation to be an instantly recognizable case of a prophet not being honored in is country which, I believe, calls for the question: One would ask who is in charge, the Pope or his commissioner?

Chapter 20

Global Warmth

I have unyielding disagreement about the theory in favor of global warming. My argument is based on the universal estimate about the size of the earth and the undeniable frictional outcome of its rotation and the revolution.

The Bermuda Triangle covers approximately 500,000 square miles in the region of the northwestern Atlantic Ocean. It covers between Bermuda, San Juan Puerto Rico, and south east of Miami Florida. There has not been any specific number of missing vessels and their crews in the Bermuda Triangle ever. The statistics differs with authors.

The Dragon's Triangle or the Devil's Sea, located off the coast of Japan is said to have more mysterious vessel disappearances than the Bermuda Triangle. American and Japanese warships, including airplanes, and Soviet nuclear missile and submarines were among the few revealed signs of wreckages in the area. In 1950, Japanese officials declared the triangle a danger zone for shipping. In 1952 a research vessel, the "Kaio Maru No. 5," which was sent by the Japanese government to investigate the troubled waters, vanished without a trace, and 22 crewmen and nine scientists were lost.

Based on the elementary hypothesis that 'nature abhors vacuum,' I affirm that global warming is fiction rather than factual for the following reasons:

First, the earth consists of 3/4 water and 1/4 of land area. And the largest parts of those lands are in Asia and Africa. Therefore if we think that man's activities are contributing to global warming, the continent of Asia and Africa are the place to start the campaign for reduction of green gas emission. The burning of bushes in Africa is common practice in their methods of farming and if we're to make any progress toward the ladder something has to be done about it along with Asian population and its industry.

Let's look at all the various sources of heat on the Earth's surface as well as the central part of the Earth—the equator; the rotation and the revolution of the Earth, the radiation of heat from the ocean floor; human and animal activities, and the influence of the sun in totality. If the climate change is not a natural phenomenon, man's effect on the physiological revolution is highly politicized and largely overestimated.

In assumption that the reduction of the rainforests, the continued growth in hydrocarbon industries, in addition to the increase in livestock, and depletion of the ozone layer are the major factors in the global warming theory, those blaming it on man's activities have carefully avoided the inclusion of toxic elements from the destructive missiles and the numerous improvised explosive devices (IED) used in battlefields around the world. The emissions of gas by aircrafts have also not been highlighted.

Breeding doomsday scenarios based on speculation and without irrefutable scientific backing is to say the least, unfair to the society.

Our elementary knowledge of geography reveals that massive coverage of the sea has vast influence on the land. Therefore it is common sense that no matter how much industrial gas is emitted into the atmosphere, the sea neutralizes it in the same way water extinguishes wild fire.

The gyratory earth neutralizes any toxic effect of escaping gases, which again, takes us back to nature's repugnance of vacuum.

If the theory about the spherical nature of the earth is to be taken into account, a spherical object as the Earth cannot produce a triangular structure. We know that other planetary bodies: sun, the Mercury, Venus, and the smallest bodies like the comets and even the Sedna—a red planetary body discovered in 2003 and is estimated to be about half the size of Pluto are all spherical. As each of these planets has circular shapes; therefore the illusion of the Bermuda Triangle is discernibly flat wrong. It should be called the Bermuda Circle.

The Journal of Quantitative Spectroscopy and Radioactive Transfer, volume 83, Issues 3-4, of February 1, 2004, Pages 377-385, reveals that elemental composition of cement kiln dust, raw materials, and cement from coal-fired factories are sources of radioactive emission. It is doubtful if pollution of the sort can go round the world. But it can have temporary localized effect in the same way as snow or rain.

Technically, with the ratio of land to the sea it doesn't matter the amount of gas emission from factories around the world the effect should be seen as a drop of water in the ocean.

From another stand point, the ozone layer, which is within the stratosphere, differs with different areas, the highest concentration measuring about 15-30km above the Earth's surface. The good news is that nature neutralizes gas emissions in such a natural and timely manner, the filtration of which falls back to Earth through precipitations.

In her comments about Global Warming, the concerns toward our children's success, in addition to too many trans-fat, carbohydrates, and the absence of a good night's sleep, Nan-Kirsten Forte, MS, executive vice president of WebMD magazine of July/August 2007, states we can not control everything.

In supporting her views, I argue, global warming is, so infinitesimal and by all standards, a natural phenomenon that has its origin, objective, function, limitations, and duration, all of which are immeasurably bigger than what humans can manipulate. Is it possible to effect a meaningful change in the coldness or hotness of the temperature in New York? If anyone thinks that is possible, we'll be thrilled about how humans can also stop the rain from falling and the sun from shining. What about preventing the ocean current? We may try, but we cannot control everything.

Each year in Chicago, during the St. Patrick's Day festival, the Irish festival organizers dye the Chicago River green, to mark the celebration. It is spectacular to watch and it's one of the things that I miss in Chicago.

Behind their celebration and tradition, we are told that the Irish thank their god for not been English or British.

In 1962, they used 100 lbs. of green dye to make the color last for a week. These days the city has cut it down to 40 pounds of food coloring to keep the river green for a couple of days before it disappears, draining itself into Lake Michigan—a much larger body of water that dissipates the green coloring.

Naturally, the total volume of water, air and space act as diluents to the total amount of pollution discharged in our environments. In other words, all toxic substances—liquids and solids in one way or the other find their resting places within the bowels of our oceans.

For example, in different places and at different times, we have oil and chemical spills in the ocean, sometimes by ocean- going vessels or oil pipelines. The effect of the spills is localized. Seaweeds and creatures may die as a result of the pollution in a given place. Eventually, the contaminants fritter away by natural balance of the larger portion of the Earth's surrounding.

Hypothetically, three houses A, B, and C are located in varying distances from one another: House 'B' is 10 ft from house 'A' and house 'C' 30 miles from 'B.' If house 'A' is on fire, the likelihood that people in house 'B' would suffer carbon monoxide from house 'A' is 100%, which makes evacuation from house 'B' absolutely necessary.

Furthermore, house "B" is in danger of burning because of its proximity to house "A," which is in flames.

The chance that people in house "C," 30 miles away, could suffer from the fume inhalation or that the house is in danger of being engulfed is out-of-the-way. The reasons are: distance and the presence of free and constant renewable oxygenated air that stretches out 30 miles from the flaming house—"A."

In another illustration, if the universe lacked natural refining properties, the destructive effects of the atomic bombs dropped on

August 6 and 9, 1945 in the cities of Hiroshima and Nagasaki would have spread out to all parts of the globe. But that was not the case.

The ocean absorbs the amount of toxins in the atmosphere and it's credible to conclude that if the amount of the toxins in the Earth's atmosphere was overpowering, we would immediately see the consequences in dead sea creatures floating along our shores.

Conclusively, every inch of the earth is full of air and the air is the source of free oxygen gas. With the presence of vast oxygenated air masses, which are larger than the localized combustion of a house, it is therefore chemically and physiologically impossible for the house in flames to impact another house 30 miles away, either by heat, flame, or air pollution.

Second, the Earth's rotation, at the rate of about 1,670 kph not only restores day and night, but also brings the yearly seasons. Due to the colossal size of the Earth, the heat energy generated as a result of the movement of the Earth may be equal to the temperature of the sun, which is up to 6.5 million °C. Notably, some of the characteristics of planetary bodies are alike.

I think scientists are yet to come up with the specifics about the Bermuda Triangle. In my opinion, our revolving Earth is comparable to all objects in motion, like aircrafts, ships, or motor vehicles. In each of these objects there exists heat energy—a product of friction. And productions of high temperatures lead to dissemination of heat, and through human engineering, all of our aircraft engines and vehicles, and machineries have heat canals—exhaust pipes.

With reference to the physical exhaust of vehicles in mind, we may conclude that the heat produced by the planetary movements and the momentous friction of the Earth along with the laws of thermodynamics, the release of gas into the Earth's stratosphere, and the Earth's assimilation of heat from the sun, in some ways are discharged through a duct—a natural phenomenon, which, I suppose is the Bermuda Triangle and the Dragon's Triangle. My presumption is that they are not triangular, but circular—the proof is from other planetary bodies—spherical objects do not produce dissimilar structures.

It is reasonable to argue that through the movement of the Earth and its absorption of the sun's energy, a dreadful degree of heat would result and therefore must have a channel though which it dumps the frictional and the conveyed energy from the solar system.

Therefore, it is possible that the Bermuda and the Dragon's Triangles, where objects have disappeared, are the exhaust cylinders of the Earth.

If there's any scientific proof that man can stop the rotation of the Earth or the influence of the sun on Earth, than the difference of opinion about global warming would not be viewed with a magnifying glass.

Again, scientific laws or the laws of nature should not be confused with the concept of hyper speculation. For instance, with a device such as electric fan or windmill, we can easily create a provisional air stream and change its direction at will in a given place. But as far as the universal body goes, it is unattainable to either generate any form of global blustery weather and or change its trend because the globe is a place bigger than the totality of life.

With the colossal size of the Earth, the amount of friction it generates through its movement is capable of melting any object that crosses the hot cylinder. I estimate that what takes place in these two areas – the Bermuda Triangle and the Devil's Triangle – is an energy-in-energy-out process having the characteristics of thermal energy and a conductivity that is capable of melting objects such as ships and airplanes. And that accounts for the disappearances.

Therefore, I strongly believe that the Bermuda and the Dragon's Triangles must be an underwater exhaust tunnel.

It is common knowledge that the oceans cover a little more than 70 percent of the Earth's surface and so makes the waters to be the world's largest solar energy collector and energy- storage organism. The energy-in-and-energy-out process is the physiological process that sustains our planet Earth; doing anything to the contrary would be counterproductive.

Analytically, the hypothesis of global warming has all the credentials of science fiction.

Do you remember the needless hysteria caused by the Y2K bug? It was a bold robbery by the software industries. An editorial writing in the Wall Street Journal called Y2K an end-of-the-world cult and the hoax of the century.

The United States spent over 300 billion dollars in response to the fraud by the software industries.

Countries like Russia, Italy and China defied the panic spending and their computers never crashed.

We track records, write history, and read history to guide and improve our present for a better tomorrow; apparently the world is not taking precaution from the events of the past.

Not long after the Y2K blunder, came the WMD (weapons of mass destruction fiasco). If those things were not enough for us to hallucinate about, America is once again propagating and promoting the tenuous seeds of global warming in broad daylight. And if this doesn't jolt the minds of scientists and anthropologist, I don't know what else would.

Chapter 21

Energy and Economics

To hammer one side of a piece of metal to straighten it does cause the opposite side of the metal to stick out. I see a wave of apprehension passing through the oil producing nations as the United States prepares to go energy independent.

We of the United States should be ready, more than ever before to giving aid and assistance, especially to the oil-producing nations that would be impoverished the more, as soon as we stop our dependency on foreign oil.

Albert Einstein, a Jewish descent, born in Germany and known for his general theory of connections between space and time, matter and energy once said, "Imagination is more important than knowledge. For while knowledge defines all we currently know and understand, imagination points to all we might yet discover and create."

As far as the alternate energy production goes, I foresee chaos and collapse of nations that are solely dependent on oil revenue. There will be untold rebellion in the oil-producing countries, and that will eventually consume American sympathy and involvement in aid and diplomatic process. The time for precaution is now.

All the troubled nations of the world have the root causes of their insecurity and lawlessness tied to the production and inequitable distribution of their oil wealth. Unfortunately, instead of utilizing their oil revenue for mechanized agriculture and set up infrastructures to provide mass employment to countless number of the population, they think that oil is the be-all and end-all of their economic and social needs.

From economic principles, it's absolutely unrealistic for any nation with a homogeneous culture to achieve healthy economic growth with out diversification.

In any highly populated country, not many people can work in the complicated oil industries. Other drawbacks of monoculture include bigger exposure to inflation, environmental health hazards, and social unrest that tick like a time bomb.

Therefore, to choose problem prevention over problem solving by organizing frequent seminars moderated by the G-8 is likely to reorganize the planning and implementation of militaristic nations to diversify their economy.

Above all, we should not forget that the only engine to a sustainable economic development in Africa is no other than a reliable and dependable power supply, whereby meat and fish products, medicines, body specimens, and reagents for hospital laboratory tests and analysis, will ensure viable infection control.

The G8 nations of Canada, France, Germany, Italy, Japan, Russia, United Kingdom, and the United States aid to Africa will succeed if they take up that giant energy project alone, for whatever good things we build end up building us.

To a large extent this will forestall rebellion and light up progress and prosperity of the nations that have not enjoyed the elements and characteristics of peaceful existence and governance.

In contrast, to give $50billion-$60 billion in aid to the third world, while allowing more billions of stolen money to rest in foreign banks is a double standard and has so far not helped the situation of the developing nations. What result are we expecting, being accomplices?

African elected officials: presidents, vice presidents, senators, and governors, including local government chairpersons are so corrupt that they transfer about two-thirds of their nation's budget into their personal foreign bank accounts.

Whereas corrupt officials in America are prosecuted imprisoned and made to refund their ill-gotten money, their African counterparts are allowed to walk the streets.

It is immoral, the banks know it; the security agents even know better; and certainly the governments of Canada, France, Germany, Italy, Japan, United Kingdom, and United States are all aware that their nations harbor the loot of the third-world countries and do nothing about it.

One question that comes to mind is: If the vision and the mission of the G8 is to enhance civilization, why are the third world nations excluded from being active members of the organization?

The G8 rule that the European Union should only be represented as an observer, but cannot chair or host the summit is outrageous of the union.

Therefore, the exclusion of the third world in global economic seminars by the G8 is, to the best of my knowledge, unhealthy and as inexcusably counterproductive as it's inequitable.

We need a new world of inclusion because the exclusion has not worked out very well in the global economy. It's better, we're told, to teach people to fish, than give them fishes.

It is better to encourage the third world to invest in its people and economy than harbor their loot. It will serve them better than the billions of dollars in the so-called aids that we pump into black holes.

Let's assume the third world is our backyard; we ought to drill the oil with our eyes open to the hazards of our oil-polluted backyard. The people in who's backyard we drill oil and produce gas need not only equipments, but also technical know-how and environmental education to live as humans, and to help save the planet.

Hope begets hope; America sets the pace for the rest of the world to follow. President Bill Clinton has shown concern in helping the third world with his Global Initiative Foundation.

With all the energy and enthusiasm behind President Obama, we hope he uses Clinton's foundation and reach out to educate Africans to adopt transparent governance in place of corruption, which has for decades handcuffed the continent from growth and expansion amid her natural resources and inexpensive labor.

We shouldn't forget that a candle loses nothing by lighting another candle—and that all eyes are on us.

Acknowledgements

My special thanks to the love of my life, BC, for her faithful support and extraordinary patience with my late night schedule while doing this work.

To my mother, Felicia Igbokwe, for teaching me not to be scapegoat amongst my peers, growing up. To my father, Stephen Igbokwe, in whose blessed memories, I owe my journal keeping guidance and his priceless advice for me not to let the things I cannot do interfere with what I can accomplish; all gave me the strength I needed to make this book possible.

To my children, Udochi, Ozi, and especially Udodi and Stephanie, who constantly gave me quiet room to organize my work and brought me tea when I needed a brake.

To everyone whose contributions have helped me to deliver this piece to my audience: Jude Onyenwe, Fr. Innocent A. Emechete, Coleman Nwachukwu and Edward Echebiri.

Finally, I am deeply grateful to my diligent and gifted editor, Mike Liechty.